RADICLIEVERS

The Baptist way of being the church

Paul Beasley-Murray

**with a Foreword by David Coffey,
General Secretary of The Baptist Union of Great Britain**

Illustrations by Linda Francis

Published by
The Baptist Union of Great Britain
November 1992

All Scripture quotations in this publication, unless otherwise stated, are from
the HOLY BIBLE, NEW INTERNATIONAL VERSION.
Copyright © 1973, 1978, 1984 by International Bible Society.

Designed, typeset and produced for the Baptist Union of Great Britain by
Gem Publishing Company, Brightwell, Wallingford, Oxfordshire.

Printed in Great Britain by Swindon Press Limited, Swindon

CONTENTS

FOREWORD

The question of identity should be on the agenda wherever Baptists gather. This may not be a fashionable issue and many will challenge it as outmoded and irrelevant. But I eagerly support those prophetic voices which see such a debate not as a revival of denominationalism but as a renewal of Baptist people in their mission. We have been robbed of our distinctive identity and a new generation needs to restore this identity with the conviction that we are not building a Baptist empire for the twenty-first century but rather are dealing with Gospel, Church and Kingdom issues in ways which justify our description as *Radical Believers*.

This is a timely book and deserves the widest circulation. Paul Beasley-Murray is well qualified to address the subjects he raises. He is a conviction Baptist who has consistently called for change and reform. He will not expect his readers to agree with all his conclusions. The purpose of the book is best discovered by engaging honestly with the issues chapter by chapter.

I hope that *Radical Believers* will be used in a variety of situations.

It should be studied by those in leadership positions in the local church. There is often a rich diversity when former Anglicans, Methodists, Roman Catholics, members of the Salvation Army, Pentecostals, Brethren and Independent Evangelicals find themselves serving on the same Baptist diaconate! I issue the challenge to such diaconates to discover the roots of our distinctive Baptist faith and tradition.

Worship styles and the concept of authority have been contentious matters for many of our local churches in recent years. *Radical Believers* raises important questions which could prove pastorally helpful if used imaginatively with house groups and church meetings.

Whatever our stance on ecumenical relations, a Baptist apologetic is needed and there are sections in the book which provide such material.

Don't overlook the international dimension to this book. In Appendix B you can read the Hoddesdon Statement on Baptist Identity which was issued during the European Baptist Federation Council in September 1992. With Europe on the agenda politically and socially, we need to strengthen our fellowship links with European Baptists and explore the development of a common identity.

I have long held the conviction that a proper understanding of Baptist identity influences the renewal of Association life and the releasing of much needed resources for Baptist mission.

This is the importance that I attach to this book, and warmly commend it in the hope that it will foster a new generation of radical believers.

David Coffey
General Secretary
The Baptist Union of Great Britain

PREFACE

I am grateful to the Baptist Union of Great Britain for entrusting me with the challenging task of writing *Radical Believers*. In this regard I wish to put on record my gratitude to David Coffey, the General Secretary, for his personal encouragement throughout the project.

A particular word of appreciation needs to be expressed to Paul Mortimore of the Ministry Department, who has given of himself unstintingly to the time-consuming task of preparing *Radical Believers* for publication. As an author I have found it a joy to work with him, and gladly acknowledge his unfailing courtesy and helpfulness at every stage. The attractive presentation of this book is very much to his credit.

Finally, in our Silver Wedding year I wish to thank the Robert Hall Society (the Cambridge University Baptist Students' Society) for introducing Caroline to me, and providing me with a most stimulating radical believer as wife.

Paul Beasley-Murray
October 1992

INTRODUCTION

RETURNING TO OUR ROOTS

In ideal terms the Baptist way of being the church is God's way for his people to live their life together. I say 'in ideal terms' because Baptists never reach the ideal. Through foolishness and sinfulness, Baptists, like their fellow Christians, fail one another and fail their Lord. Nonetheless Baptists claim that their study of God's Word leads them to believe that there is a pattern for their corporate life in Christ, and that the Baptist way of being the church is modelled on that pattern.

For many people in Baptist churches in Britain this may come as a surprise. For them being a Baptist is just one of many possible ways of being a Christian. Indeed, many people join our churches not because they wish to become Baptists, but rather because they wish to become members of a particular local church, which happens to be Baptist. They are attracted initially, not by the congregation's theology of the church, but by other factors: the preaching and teaching, the worship, the fellowship, the range of activities for children and young people. The Baptist way of being the church is secondary – if not irrelevant – to these other considerations.

This study guide is written from the conviction that theology (the way we think about God and associated themes) is important. Moreover, the application of that theology to our understanding of the church (ecclesiology) is important. The Baptist way of being the church is not just one of several options open to us. Our study of God's Word leads us to believe that this is God's way for living our life together. It is in this sense that Baptists are radical believers. For Baptists believe in getting back to the roots of the Christian faith (note that the English word 'radical' is derived from the Latin word 'radix', which means 'root'). We seek to root our life together in the Word of God.

BAPTIST DISTINCTIVES

But is there a specific Baptist way of being the church? There is an old joke that for every hundred Baptists there are a hundred different opinions! Certainly Baptists are not monochrome, and a wide variety of views are found amongst them. Yet for all their variety, Baptists share certain distinctives which make them Baptist.

There is no one distinctive Baptist belief. Although probably most people think of believers' baptism as the primary Baptist distinctive, Baptists are not the only Christians to practise believers' baptism – Pentecostals, for example, also practise it. Another key Baptist distinctive is the concept of congregational church government – a concept shared, as the term implies, by Congregationalists and some other Christian churches. Likewise, other important Baptist distinctives, such as the priesthood of all believers or the separation of church and state, are not peculiar to Baptists. It is the combination of these various beliefs which makes Baptists distinctive. Perhaps Baptist distinctives may be likened to a set of genes which, because of their particular arrangement, produce a family likeness wherever they are found.

Baptists tend to jump from the New Testament to the present day, forgetting that as heirs of the radical reformation they have a noble history.

Baptists need to remember that it was they who championed the cause of religious freedom, spearheaded the modern missionary movement, and, along with other Christians, kept alive the evangelical flame of faith. Appendix A on page 112 provides a brief account of the Baptist story.

The book begins by looking at **believers' baptism**, with its emphasis on the need for personal faith in Christ. This commitment to Christ and his people, inherent in baptism, also receives expression in **the Lord's Supper** – the other main ordinance of the church. This leads us on to look in general at how Baptists approach **worship**, with their emphasis on the preaching of the Word.

The Baptist way of being the church emphasises the importance of 'covenant' relationships: we therefore examine what this commitment to one another means in terms of **church membership**.

Linked to church membership is the Baptist understanding of **authority**, with its emphasis on the **church meeting** as the place where with God's help all important decisions are made. In spite of this emphasis on the church meeting, however, Baptists believe not in independency but inter-dependency: hence for them the importance of **associating** with other Baptists and with other Christians.

The last two distinctives relate to the Baptist understanding of **ministry**, with an emphasis on the ministry of every member; and the Baptist commitment to **mission**, with an emphasis on personal evangelism.

These distinctives together make Baptists Baptist. They are distinctives without which the wider church of God would be much the poorer, and to which Baptists still need to bear witness.

DENOMINATIONS UNDER FIRE

But is Baptist identity really still worth fighting for? Is it still important for Baptists to maintain their way of being the church? Some think not and are critical of denominations in general:

'Denominations are counter to the will of God', say some independents. In a sense that is true. Nobody pretends that a Church divided into Anglicans, Baptists, Lutherans, and Roman Catholics, together with a host of other group-ings, expresses perfectly the will of God. But the creation of independent, non-denominational 'fellowships' does not solve the problem. If anything, it increases the range of choice, and baffles the outsider even more.

'Denominations have had their day', say some deeply committed to the ecumenical cause. But the interests of unity are not furthered by a disregard of biblical truths which denominations have preciously safeguarded down the centuries. It is increasingly recognised that unity in terms of uniformity is not an option. The way forward is for the denominations to recognise their unity in spite of their diversity.

'Denominations have the hand of death on them', say some restorationists, as if the life of the Spirit is in their churches and nowhere else.

Some churches are more dead than alive, but to write off entire denominations on that basis is to grieve the Spirit. In all denominations there is life, and to pretend that only one group of churches contains the life of the Spirit is unjustified spiritual arrogance.

Others are critical of Baptists in particular:

'Not all Baptist churches preach the gospel', say some of our critics. So much depends, of course, on what we mean by 'the gospel'. In a way which is not true of other mainline churches, Baptist churches are by and large evangelical. Some perhaps are less willing to dot 'i's and cross 't's than others, but at the end of the day we all have to recognise that God's truth is bigger than any of our perceptions. The fact is that believers' baptism ensures that the concept of conversion is at the heart of every Baptist church.

'Not all Baptist churches are alive with the Spirit', say other critics. If by that is meant that not all Baptists 'swing from the chandeliers' in worship, then certainly that is true. In many places, however, Baptist churches have been marked by fresh life and growth. Honesty compels us to recognise that there are churches which appear to go through the motions, and no more. But experience shows that where lively Christians are prepared to put their backs into such churches, renewal and reformation is possible from within.

'**Baptist churches have less evangelistic potential**', say others, who join the state church where they believe there is a 'bigger pond in which to fish'. But is evangelistic pragmatism to outweigh allegiance to theological truth? If pragmatism is a factor, then there are good pragmatic reasons today for being a Baptist. In the closing decade of the second millenium, Baptists as a denomination are well placed to take advantage of gospel opportunities afforded by this crucial turning-point in world history.

For most people, in practice, the choice is not between differing denominations and theologies, but between individual churches and what they have to offer. People today change denominations less out of theological conviction and more out of personal interest and convenience. The philosophy of the consumer society and its emphasis upon choice holds sway. People choose a church because of what it offers; its worship, teaching and range of activities. Theology and any particular doctrine of the church (ecclesiology) are relatively unimportant.

But matters relating to theology and ecclesiology *are* important – for both are expressions of Christian truth as revealed in God's Word, the Bible. Theological conviction – and not just personal convenience – has a role to play for the 'Bible-believing' Christian. The Bible is not just about personal faith, it is also about the corporate expression of that faith. At that point the Baptist way of being the church immediately becomes relevant, for it is a way of life rooted in Scripture. Radical believing is not the prerogative of the rugged individualist, it involves a corporate life among the people of God. Baptists, with their emphasis on the believers' church, dare to believe that their way of being the church is consistent with God's pattern of life for his people as found within the pages of the New Testament.

There will always be valid pastoral reasons for certain individuals switching from a Baptist church to one of another denomination, where they may receive the help and teaching they need. Generally, however, such a switch is regrettable. If for any reason a Baptist church appears not to bear all the marks of a church that is alive and well, then surely the person who has entered into a covenant relationship with fellow Baptist believers should seek the renewal and reform of that church from within.

A PERSONAL TESTIMONY

Let me conclude this introduction with a personal testimony. Although brought up within a Baptist home, I agreed to write this book on Baptist identity because I have become a Baptist by conviction. From a study of the Scriptures I am convinced that the Baptist way of being the church is God's pattern for his people's life together. This does not mean that either I or my fellow Baptists have always lived out that pattern. But by theological conviction, expressed in baptism and church membership, this is the family to which I belong and in which I therefore shall stay. But thank God, this covenant is not one way. My experience is that as I have sought to honour this covenant, in turn others have honoured their side of the covenant by their love and acceptance of me. It is therefore a family which on experiential, as well as theological, grounds I delight to commend to others.

I
Confessing the Faith
– the baptism of believers only –

THE CENTRALITY OF CONVERSION

A frequent fun slogan on Christian tee-shirts used to be the line, 'Baptists are wet all over'. In the eyes of many, baptism by total immersion is the key Baptist distinctive – and hence the name. Although, perhaps understandably, it is the dramatic act of baptism which visitors to our services remember, for Baptists themselves it is the quality of faith – rather than the quantity of water – which ultimately counts. In the first place Baptists practise *believers'* baptism.

This emphasis on *believers'* baptism is sometimes misunderstood by other Christians, who speak of Baptists practising *adult* baptism over against infant baptism. This, however, is not an exact contrast. Baptists do not baptise adults *per se*. Indeed, many baptismal candidates are young people who have yet to attain their formal majority. What counts is not age but faith. Adults and young people alike are baptised – as believers.

A theology of conversion is at the heart of the Baptist understanding of baptism. Baptism expresses the believer's response of faith to the grace of God. Or to put it another way, on theological grounds it may be truer to say that believers' baptism stems from the Baptist model of a believers' church, and in many ways therefore the latter, rather than the former, is our key distinctive.

Thus, over against the great state churches of Europe, Baptists developed a radical model of the church, where faith in Jesus as expressed through baptism is the means of entry. (Look at Appendix A, page 113, for more on the idea of a state church. After Constantine a view of the church emerged which saw every citizen, because baptised as an infant, as a member of the church.)

> **TO THINK ABOUT . . .**
> How have you answered in the past when asked what is distinctive about Baptist beliefs?
>
> At the end of the book you will have opportunity to come back to the question to see if you have revised your answer.

THE BASIS FOR BAPTISM

Baptists frequently offer three reasons for their practice of baptism:

THE COMMAND OF CHRIST

The first and ultimately the most powerful reason for baptism is found in the Great Commission. Jesus, as he was about to ascend to his Father, declared:

All authority in heaven and on earth has been given to me. Therefore go and make disciples of all nations, baptising them in the name of the Father and of the Son and of the Holy Spirit, and teaching them to obey everything I have commanded you.

And surely I will be with you always, to the very end of the age (Matt 28:18–20).

Jesus here issues a command, whose validity does not expire until 'the very end of the age'. Baptism is therefore no optional extra, but an observance ordained by Christ for all who would be his disciples.

The fact that we are dealing with a command of Christ deals with the not infrequent objection raised by some that they do not yet 'feel' it right to be baptised. Baptism is not dependent on feelings, it is in the first place an act of obedience. If we love Jesus, we will want to obey him. Indeed, on another occasion, Jesus said to his disciples: 'You are my friends if you do what I command' (John 15:14). Baptism is a necessary part of the discipleship process.

The authenticity of Matthew 28:18–20 has been questioned by some, but the dictum of the distinguished New Testament scholar, Ethelbert Stauffer, should be noted:

> How this Christian practice of baptism originated is a puzzle that only begins to be solved if we come at last once more to conclude that the tradition of the Risen Lord giving a missionary charge is to be taken seriously.

'I know I was a teenage convert, but I needed time to think about baptism.'

Baptism, then, marks the beginning of the discipleship process. 'Baptism' does not follow 'teaching', but rather 'teaching' follows 'baptism'. This does not do away with the Baptist practice of baptismal classes, where the significance of baptism is spelled out to the enquirer. It does, however, raise a question mark over any lengthy interval, perhaps of several years, between conversion and baptism. From a New Testament point of view, baptism belongs to the conversion process. We are not truly committed to Jesus until we have committed ourselves to him in the waters of baptism.

THE EXAMPLE OF CHRIST

Popular thinking sometimes views Christ's example, in being baptised himself, as reinforcing his command (see Matt 3:13–17; Mark 1:9–11; Luke 3:21–22). It is argued that if Jesus himself was baptised, then we should be too. Attention is drawn to Jesus' reply to John: 'Let it be so now; it is proper for us to do this to fulfil all righteousness', or as the Goods News Bible puts it, 'for in this way we shall do all that God requires' (Matt 3:15).

However, the parallel is not as close as might initially appear. Jesus, 'a lamb without blemish or defect' (1 Pet 1:19), did not submit himself to baptism to wash his sins away, but rather took his first step to the Cross by identifying himself with us in our sin*ful*ness. By contrast, in baptism we identify ourselves with Jesus in his sin*less*ness!

A better parallel is that we, like Jesus, must be prepared to submit ourselves to the will of God and 'do what God requires'. A further parallel may be that, just as baptism marked the beginning of Jesus' ministry, so our baptism marks the beginning of our service for God.

THE PRACTICE OF THE EARLY CHURCH

A further basis for baptism is that the first Christians took this command of Jesus seriously. We see this on the day of Pentecost. Luke tells us that when the people heard Peter's sermon:

> they were cut to the heart and said to Peter and the other apostles, 'Brothers, what shall we do?'. Peter

replied, 'Repent and be baptised, every one of you, in the name of Jesus Christ so that your sins may be forgiven. And you will receive the gift of the Holy Spirit (Acts 2:37–38).

Part of the process of becoming a Christian was being baptised.

> **TO THINK ABOUT . . .**
> **Should Baptists call people to be baptised at the same time as they make evangelistic appeals, calling people to repentance and faith in Jesus Christ?**

As we examine the Acts of the Apostles, it becomes clear that baptism was an integral part of the conversion process.

- A large number of Samaritans (Acts 8:11–13) and later the Ethiopian finance minister (Acts 8:26–40) came to faith in Christ and were baptised by Philip.
- Paul was baptised by Ananias after meeting Jesus on the Damascus Road (Acts 9:10–19; 22:12–16).
- Cornelius and his friends were baptised by Peter, following the gift of the Spirit (Acts 10:44–48).
- Lydia, the dealer in purple goods (Acts 16:13–15), and the Philippian jailer (Acts 16:25–34) were both baptised by Paul as part

of their response to the Christian gospel, as were Crispus and many of his fellow Corinthians (Acts 18:8).
- Paul baptised the Ephesian disciples of John the Baptist (Acts 19:1–7), after they had come to a clearer understanding of Jesus.

All these instances reveal that baptism was part of the process of becoming a Christian. Indeed, it is no exaggeration to say that in New Testament times there came to be no such person as an unbaptised Christian. Paul could write to the Corinthians: 'We were *all* baptised' (1 Cor 12:13). The only exceptions to this generalisation were the apostles themselves, who at the beginning had probably only known the baptism of John.

> **TO THINK ABOUT . . .**
> **In the light of the close link between baptism and conversion in the early church, should we expect today to see people baptised on the day they come to faith? Do Baptists need to become more radical in their approach to Scripture on this matter?**
>
> **What are the arguments for and against a lengthy period, maybe several weeks or months, of instruction before baptism?**
>
> **In living memory in Zaire a candidate often had to be able to read before being baptised. Why do you think this practice was adopted and was it a good practice?**

THE SIGNIFICANCE OF BAPTISM

Baptism is multifaceted, and rich in symbolism. From a New Testament perspective it has a five-fold meaning.

A DECLARATION OF UNION WITH CHRIST

Baptism is a dramatic way of declaring our solidarity with Jesus, crucified and risen. It is the moment when a believer expresses his or her union with Christ. Paul put it this way:

don't you know that all of us who were baptised into Christ Jesus were baptised into his death? We were therefore buried with him through baptism into death in order that, just as Christ was raised from the dead through the glory of the Father, we too may live a new life (Rom 6:3–4; similarly Col 2:12).

The imagery here is that of a watery grave in which baptismal candidates, as they go under the water, identify themselves with the Christ who died for them, and as they rise up out of the

ST. AGNES' BAPTISES INFANTS BY IMMERSION

'Darling, the vicar wants to see Jeremy's Grade 2 survival certificate.'

water they identify themselves with the Christ who rose for them. In baptism they are in effect saying – 'Yes Lord, you died for me'; 'Yes Lord, you rose for me'.

But baptism is far more than a credal statement. It has ethical implications also: baptism is a dying to the old way of living and a rising to Christ's new way of living. To declare solidarity with Christ, and in this way to identify with him and with him alone, is a revolutionary act. It is an acknowledgement of the lordship of Christ, come hell or high water. To die to self is to die to the old way of living. It is to turn from sin and to renounce evil. Baptism is more than a mere act of obedience. It involves total surrender to Christ. What is more, this surrender is a surrender of a life-time. From this point on there is no going back. As with Christian marriage, so too with baptism, the relationship entered into is for life. The union is to be indissoluble.

> **TO THINK ABOUT . . .**
>
> **Is the revolutionary nature of what you commit yourself to in believers' baptism a good reason for allowing time for instruction and preparation before you make this 'surrender of a life-time'?**
>
> **If you have been baptised, does your own experience of baptism help you answer this question?**

All this is symbolised in the waters of baptism. It is precisely this understanding of dying and rising with Christ which demands total immersion. Interestingly, even the Anglican *Book of Common Prayer* recognises that immersion is the norm, and offers affusion ('sprinkling') only as an alternative where a baby is sickly. However, in the Orthodox tradition the biblical symbolism is retained and babies are immersed in the font.

Baptists differ in how precisely they immerse. Most commonly, candidates are taken backwards into the water as a sign of burial. However, in parts of Africa candidates are baptised by being plunged down into the water – a meaningful symbol where people are buried vertically! An alternative mode is to have candidates kneel in the water, then take them forwards as a sign of their submission to Christ.

A SIGN OF CLEANSING

Another Scriptural way of understanding baptism is to see it as a 'bath' in which our sins are washed away. This symbolism, also apparent in the form of baptism practised by John the Baptist, is found in a number of Scripture passages.

Acts 22:16

Ananias said to Paul: 'And now what are you waiting for? Get up, be baptised and wash your sins away, calling on his name.' The link between the 'washing' and the 'calling on the name of Jesus' is significant: the water alone does not cleanse.

Ephesians 5:25–27

We find in this passage a similar link between 'washing' and 'the word', although scholars are uncertain whether 'the word' in question is a reference to the preaching of the gospel or a confession of faith.

Titus 3:5

Paul here also describes baptism as 'the washing of rebirth'. Although there is no reference to faith in this particular passage, in another of his 'Pastoral Letters' Paul quotes an early Christian baptismal hymn which emphasises the need for those who have 'died' with Christ in baptism to 'endure' in the faith (2 Tim 2:11–13).

Hebrews 10:22

The writer to the Hebrews exhorts his readers to 'draw near to God . . . having our hearts sprinkled to cleanse us from a guilty conscience and having our bodies washed with pure water'. The external cleansing is a sign of an internal cleansing.

As Peter makes clear, it is not the water itself which removes the 'dirt' of this life, but rather 'the God and Father of our Lord Jesus Christ' who in his mercy gives 'new birth' to those who respond in faith to his grace through baptism: 'baptism', he declares, 'now saves you – not [as] the removal of dirt from the body but [as] the pledge of a good conscience toward God', or as the Good News Bible puts it, 'as the promise made to God from a good conscience' (1 Pet 1:3–5; 3:21).

This aspect of baptism reminds us that all of us need to be cleansed by the blood of Jesus (see 1 John 1:8–9). Strangely one sometimes comes across people who delay their baptism on the ground that they are not yet good enough for God – as if baptism is some special sign of Christian maturity. The reverse is surely the case. In baptism we acknowledge that we are *not* good enough – that we stand in need of Christ's cleansing power. Indeed, the moment that we think we are good enough for God, that moment we are not fit to be baptised. Baptism is for sinners – albeit penitent sinners – only.

TO THINK ABOUT . . .
Caroline, Alison and Kevin were fielding questions at the youth group one Sunday evening, after a service of believers' baptism. The service had clearly made a big impression on the young people. Some of them hadn't been to such a service before, so the questions and comments came thick and fast.

Josh, who had been attending the evening service for several months, finally got a word in.

'I couldn't do what they did tonight. To start with I'm not good enough to be baptised. Perhaps I will one day, when I'm good enough.'

If you were Caroline, Alison or Kevin, how would you reply to Josh?

A CONFESSION OF FAITH

When Paul wrote to the church at Rome, 'If you confess with your mouth "Jesus is Lord", and believe in your heart that God raised him from the dead, you will be saved' (Rom 10:9), he almost certainly had the act of baptism in mind. In the New Testament, baptism is the great moment when Christians nail their colours to the mast and declare that they belong to Christ and to his people. Thus it is generally agreed that Paul is referring to baptism when he writes to Timothy: 'Take hold of the eternal life to which you were called when you made your good confession in the presence of many witnesses' (1 Tim 6:12).

Most Baptists feel happiest with this aspect of baptism, after viewing it first and foremost as an act of witness. To this end, it is customary in many Baptist churches for baptismal candidates to give personal 'testimonies' to God's saving power in their own lives: for, although baptism itself is a confession of faith, it is considered good to give opportunity for candidates to articulate this confession and tell of what Christ means to them. Again, it is customary in many Baptist churches for the candidates to invite friends and relatives to their baptism, in order to share their testimony beyond the church. Baptism can never be a private affair.

> **TO THINK ABOUT . . .**
>
> It could be argued that modern baptistries are an unfortunate compromise: a river or lake is so much more public!
>
> Do you agree? Have you evidence of anyone coming to faith in Christ through seeing another person baptised or confessing his or her faith in a testimony?
>
> What do you learn from your answer?

A RITE OF INITIATION

From a New Testament perspective baptism is the normal way of entering the church. 1 Corinthians 12:13 leads clearly to this conclusion: 'For we were all baptised by one Spirit into one body.' Similar thinking underlies Galatians 3:26–28, where Paul's mention of faith leads him on to baptism which in turn leads him on to speak of the church:

> In Christ Jesus you are all children of God through faith. As many of you as were baptised into Christ have clothed yourselves with Christ. There is no longer Jew or Greek, there is no longer slave or free, there is no longer male or female; for you are all one in Christ Jesus (NRSV).

The actual word 'church' may be missing, but a sense of Christian community into which believers' baptism leads is very much present. In baptism we commit ourselves not simply to Christ, but also to the people of Christ.

Sadly, many Baptists in Britain have not always seen baptism as a rite of initiation. They have individualised the rite to such an extent that sometimes it is simply an act of witness and nothing more. In a good number of English Baptist churches it is possible to be baptised and yet not become a church member. It may be that some reform of baptismal practice is necessary to ensure that only in exceptional cases – for example, where someone from a church practising infant baptism wishes to be baptised as a believer and yet remain a member of that church – would it be possible to be baptised without becoming a member of the church. For baptism is a *church* ordinance – it is not for spiritual gypsies.

> **TO THINK ABOUT . . .**
>
> What steps are taken or could be taken by your church to ensure that a new Christian does not think of baptism as merely an individual act of witness?
>
> Some Baptist churches emphasise that baptism is the door to the church by following baptism immediately with the Lord's Supper, at which the candidates are received into membership.
>
> What arguments support or cast doubts on this practice?
>
> What benefits come from unbelieving friends being present at the Lord's Supper as well as the baptism? Are there any practical or other disadvantages?

A SIGN OF THE SPIRIT'S PRESENCE

The Spirit is God's gift to all who put their trust in Jesus as their Saviour and Lord. Paul likens the Spirit to God's stamp of ownership, God's down-payment with a promise of more to come:

> Having believed, you were marked in him with a seal, the promised Holy Spirit, who is a deposit guaranteeing our inheritance until the redemption of those who are God's possession – to the praise of his glory. (Eph 1:13–14).

As in baptism we express our trust in Jesus as our Saviour and Lord, it is not surprising that baptism is associated with the gift of God's Spirit.

This association with the Spirit is seen in Peter's preaching on the Day of Pentecost:

> Repent and be baptised, every one of you, in the name of Jesus Christ so that your sins may be forgiven. And you will receive the gift of the Holy Spirit' (Acts 2:38).

The Spirit is clearly linked with baptism, and is consequent upon baptism. A similar link between baptism and the Spirit is found in the writings of Paul. To the Corinthians Paul wrote, 'you were washed, you were sanctified, you were justified in the name of the Lord Jesus Christ and by the Spirit of our God' (1 Cor 6:11), indicating that the Spirit is active not only in the process of sanctification and justification, but also in baptism.

This same activity of the Spirit in baptism is mentioned by Paul in his letter to Titus: God 'saved us through the washing of rebirth and renewal by the Holy Spirit' (Titus 3:5). Hence Paul can write: 'we were all baptised by one Spirit into one body' (1 Cor 12:13). Baptism, from a New Testament perspective, is a believer's personal Pentecost.

Is the Spirit always associated with baptism? In the Acts of the Apostles we read of two occasions when the gift of the Spirit is clearly distinguished from baptism, but these are exceptional occasions, marking two new stages in the church's mission as the gospel crosses over to both the Samaritan and Gentile worlds.

On the first occasion, the Samaritans, whom Philip had baptised, did not receive the Spirit until Peter and John arrived to pray for them: the gift of the Spirit was delayed until the official leaders of the church had acknowledged that even despised Samaritans could also belong to the new people of God (Acts 8:14–17).

On the second occasion, the Spirit falls on Cornelius and his friends even before they are baptised. As a result, Peter concludes that they should be baptised precisely because they have already received the Spirit 'just as we have' (Acts 10:46–48): God in his sovereign grace shows that even Gentiles can belong to his church. Both these cases – the so-called 'Samaritan Pentecost' and the 'Gentile Pentecost' – are exceptional. They and are not normative for Christian experience, but in different ways they testify to the inalienable link between conversion and baptism.

From a New Testament perspective, then, baptism marks a twofold commitment: we commit ourselves to God in response to his love for us expressed in Jesus, but God in turn further commits himself to us through his Spirit. Baptism is a sign of the Spirit's presence.

BAPTISM A SACRAMENT?

At this point, however, many Baptists begin to be unhappy. Traditionally Baptists have been very wary of any suggestion that God may be active in baptism. Most Baptists are happy to speak of symbolism, but are suspicious of anything that smacks of 'sacramentalism'. Any link with the Spirit is therefore often denied. For this reason many Baptists have avoided using the term 'sacrament' of baptism.

But what is a sacrament? A sacrament has been defined as 'an outward and visible sign of inward and spiritual grace'. The Roman Catholic and Orthodox churches have applied the term sacrament to the seven rites of baptism, confirmation, the Lord's Supper, penance, extreme unction, ordination, and marriage. The great Protestant churches have restricted the term to baptism and the Lord's Supper.

Baptists, however, have tended to avoid using the word sacrament because of its association at times with semi-magical ideas. Thus Henry Cook, a Baptist stalwart of an earlier generation, charged that for sacramentalists

> Baptism and the Lord's Supper were changed into mysterious rites that produced supernatural effects in those who received them, whether they had any personal faith or no.

He therefore preferred to use the traditional Baptist term 'ordinance' for baptism and the Lord's Supper, as rites which had been 'ordained' or laid down by our Lord (see Matt 28:19; 1 Cor 11:23–25).

Although Henry Cook's position is typical of most Baptists, a growing number believe that it is not good enough to refer to baptism and the Lord's Supper as rites which merely 'symbolise' the faith. They are rites in which the Spirit may be active – provided that faith is present (no Baptist accepts that baptism and the Lord's Supper have meaning where faith is absent – that is to enter the realm of magic and superstition).

TO THINK ABOUT . . .

Someone has described baptism as 'a God appointed rendez-vous'.

What does the phrase mean to you and how is it helpful in describing what happens in believers' baptism?

BAPTISM WITH THE LAYING ON OF HANDS

Baptists in Britain, in rediscovering the association of baptism with the Spirit, are increasingly bringing back the old Baptist practice of accompanying baptism with the laying on of hands. Customs vary as to when this rite is carried out. It can take place in the waters of baptism, immediately after the baptism itself. This gives a sense of immediacy. The disadvantage is that the candidate is probably still recovering from having been dipped under the water. Hence candidates are often first given time to change into dry clothes, and then are prayed for. The purpose of such prayer is to invoke the Spirit to confirm the unity of the baptised with Christ and fill the candidate with fresh power for witness and service.

TO THINK ABOUT . . .

Does the argument for laying hands on a candidate immediately after baptism outweigh any practical difficulties? Why?

THE BAPTISM OF THE HOLY SPIRIT

As a result of charismatic renewal many Baptists have become interested in the 'baptism of (or in) the Holy Spirit'. Traditionally Pentecostals have

'Pastor, don't you think you ought to let him up from the water before you lay hands on him?'

taught that the 'baptism of the Holy Spirit' is a second-stage experience for which the evidence is always speaking in tongues. There is, however, no scriptural justification for such a doctrine. True, John the Baptist spoke of Jesus as the one who would 'baptise' with the Holy Spirit (Matt 3:11; Mark 1:8; Luke 3:16; John 1:33), but this 'prophecy' received general fulfilment on the Day of Pentecost (see Acts 2:33), and continues to receive particular fulfilment each time a person comes to faith in Christ.

The only place in the New Testament letters where this metaphor comes to expression is in 1 Corinthians 12, where Paul links the reception of the Spirit with (water) baptism: 'we were all baptised by one Spirit into one body' (1 Cor 12:13). That is, baptism is 'into' Christ and 'into' the Body of Christ, and is therefore the sign of initiation into Christ and into the Body. In that context Paul makes clear that the 'baptising' Spirit bestows many and various gifts – to highlight any particular gift, and to suggest it should be universal, runs directly counter to the teaching of 1 Corinthians 12.

All this, however, is not to deny the reality of charismatic experience, but rather to challenge certain charismatic terminology. From a Scriptural point of view, the challenge of the Christian life is not so much the baptism as the 'fullness' of the Spirit. Thus in Ephesians 5:18 Paul urges us to 'be [keep on being] filled with the Spirit'. In our living we should constantly seek to open ourselves up to the presence and power of God's Spirit.

> ### TO THINK ABOUT . . .
>
> **In the New Testament not only faith and baptism but also baptism and the Spirit are linked. Here is a three-stranded cord which should not be divided.**
>
> **What practical implications arise from this understanding of baptism?**
>
> **Why do you either support or oppose the term 'sacrament' in reference to baptism and the Lord's Supper?**

BAPTISM IS FOR BELIEVERS ONLY

Baptists have always maintained that baptism is for believers only. However, as a courtesy to our 'paedobaptist' (i.e. those who baptise young children) brothers and sisters, who after all form the majority of Christians today, we should look at the arguments for infant baptism.

HOUSEHOLD BAPTISM

In ancient society the solidarity of the family was more strongly stressed than ours. Thus in Acts 11:14 (Cornelius); 16:15 (Lydia); 16:33 (the Philippian jailer); 18:8 (Crispus); and 1 Corinthians 1:16 (Stephanas) we read of the person and his or her 'house' being baptised. This, paedobaptists argue, naturally includes husband, wife and all the children.

However, the paedobaptist case is immediately weakened once it is recognised that in the first century the family extended considerably beyond parents and children to include cousins,

uncles, aunts and grandparents. Slaves were also included in the family and they formed more than half the population of the Roman empire. To assume that the term 'house' or 'family' immediately refers to little children, and even to infants, is to interpret the New Testament in terms of the Western nuclear family.

If we look at some of the references to the 'house' or 'family', with young children particularly in mind, the case for infant baptism becomes very weak. Look carefully, for instance, at the story of the Philippian jailer (Acts 16:29–34): 'Men, what must I do to be saved?', asked the jailer. 'Believe in the Lord Jesus,' replied Paul and Silas, 'and you will be saved – you and your household.' Luke tells us: 'Then they spoke the word of the Lord to him and to all the others in his house . . . then immediately he and all his family were baptised.' Now, if 'all the family' included young children, then we must believe that those children not only listened to Paul and Silas (it was gone midnight), but that they also put their trust in God!

Acts 10:44–46 and 11:14 tell how *all* the house of Cornelius heard the word, received the Spirit, spoke in tongues and were baptised: are we to believe that little children were involved in all this? Also in Acts 18:8 we read that Crispus and *all* his family *believed* and were baptised. Finally in 1 Corinthians 16:15–16 Paul urged submission to the household of Stephanas – surely this does not include children?

Jesus Christ welcomed children. In the Gospels (Mark 10:13–16; Matt 19:13–15) Jesus commands his disciples not to hinder the children from coming to him, and gives his blessing to those who came. The kingdom of heaven belongs to them, he said. This, paedobaptists argue, would therefore make it very strange to exclude children from baptism.

But this does not establish the paedobaptist case. Baptists do not doubt the love of Jesus for children and his desire to welcome them. But Jesus declared that children were models of how mature people should *receive* the Kingdom: 'anyone who will not receive the kingdom of God like a little child will never enter it' (Mark 10:15). It is childlike faith which Jesus here holds before us. This is no model for infant baptism, for in infant baptism children are entirely passive – in no way do they actively receive Christ.

TO THINK ABOUT . . .

If *infant* baptism encourages a complacency among youngsters that they are already Christians, without having to make a personal response of repentance to God and faith in Jesus, does our stress on *believers'* baptism leave us weak in understanding where children from Christian families fit into the life of a local Baptist church?

How can Baptists express more effectively God's concern for children and find a place for them in the believing community?

PROSELYTE BAPTISM

When a Gentile man was converted to Judaism (and thus became a 'proselyte'), he was required to be circumcised and baptised, and his family also submitted to initiatory rites. Baptism became important, since women and girls received it also. From this, it is argued, we can assume that the early church applied baptism in much the same way, baptising all the family, children included.

However, the following facts need to be carefully considered. Genuine uncertainty exists about whether proselyte baptism was widely known in the time of the apostles. It appears that John the Baptist provided the model for the baptismal practice which Jesus adopted. Some have thought 1 Corinthians 7:14 reflects a Christian parallel to proselyte baptism, since there Paul writes of children being 'sanctified' or 'made holy' by the faith of a parent. However, Paul also refers to the unbelieving spouse being 'sanctified' or 'made holy' – it is unlikely that the unbelieving spouse was baptised! The Jews used the expression 'sanctified' only of children born after conversion to the Jewish faith, and no baptism was then required to make the children Jewish. Clearly Paul did not apply the custom of proselyte baptism to Christian baptism.

Did you hear about the paedobaptist who got into deep water over baptism?

Hallelujah!

COVENANT AND CIRCUMCISION

Under the old covenant children born to Jewish parents were received as of right into the community almost immediately after birth. They belonged to the covenant people, the sign of which was circumcision. Under the new covenant, it is argued, children of Christian parents should similarly be received as of right into the church community, and they should receive the sign of this – baptism, which has now replaced circumcision.

There is no evidence, however, that the early church viewed baptism applied to children of Christians in the same way as circumcision was used to mark Jewish children as children of the covenant. On the contrary, in Galatians 3 Paul contrasts baptism and faith with circumcision and the law:

> The law was put in charge of us to lead us to Christ that we might be justified by faith. Now that faith has come, we are no longer under the supervision of the law. In Christ Jesus you are all children of God through faith. As many of you as were baptised into Christ have clothed yourselves with Christ.' (Galatians 3:24–27 NRSV).

Baptism was not seen as replacing circumcision, for in Acts 21:21 James and the elders of the Jerusalem church speak of the Jewish churches' right to continue the rite of circumcision.

Finally, in Colossians 2:11 the phrase 'the circumcision done by Christ' does not refer to baptism but to the death of Christ – a terrible picture because to Jews circumcision was, with the Passover, the greatest of all sacrifices. Christians do not need it, says Paul, since the great sacrifice was offered for them, the power of which they know through conversion and baptism:

> In him also you were circumcised with a spiritual circumcision, by putting off the body of flesh in the circumcision of Christ; when you were buried with him in baptism, you were also raised with him through faith in the power of God, who raised him for the dead' (Col 2:11–12 NRSV).

BAPTISM AND THE GRACE OF GOD

We consider one final argument relating to infant baptism. Infant baptism, it is sometimes maintained, glorifies the grace of God. This, the argument goes, reminds us that we are not saved because of our faith but through the gracious action of God in Christ. Indeed, to insist on the presence of faith in the baptised is said to be tantamount to denying grace and perverting the gospel!

But this argument does not do justice to the New Testament understanding of baptism. Baptism is the believer's response to the grace of God. Baptists with their Calvinistic heritage recognise that it is by grace that we have been saved, but 'through faith' (Eph 2:8). Believers' baptism is no denial of the grace of God, but involves rather a joyful acceptance of that grace.

> *TO THINK ABOUT . . .*
> **In infant baptism the peril is to see God's saving grace somehow infused into a baby who is unable to enter any meaningful relationship with God.**
>
> **How do Baptists avoid the danger of so stressing in baptism the believer's faith, decision and response that they put too little emphasis on baptism testifying to God's free and undeserved grace?**

CONCLUSION

To sum up, the 'paedobaptist' position fails to hold water! Nowhere does the New Testament implicitly assume that young children were baptised. Rather is it explicitly stated that *believers* were baptised. Time and time again, faith and baptism are clearly linked. Clear references to believers' baptism are found, for example in the following:

- Peter's appeal on the Day of Pentecost (Acts 2:38: 'Repent and be baptised, every one of you . . .');
- the Samaritan response to Philip's preaching (Acts 8:12: 'when they believed . . . they were baptised . . .');
- Peter's explanation of baptism's 'saving' power (1 Pet 3:21: 'baptism . . . now saves you also – not [as] the removal of dirt from the body but [as] the pledge of a good conscience towards God');
- Colossians 2:12 quoted above;
- Galatians 3:26–27 the statement 'You are all sons of God through faith in Christ Jesus' is immediately followed by a reference to

baptism: 'all of you who were baptised into Christ Jesus have been clothed with Christ.'

Even if we do not include the Western text reading of Acts 8:37 (where, in answer to the Ethiopian's question, 'Why shouldn't I be baptised?', Philip replies, 'If you believe with all your heart, you may'), the case is clear enough. Baptism is always accompanied by faith. Furthermore, the theology of baptism in the New Testament always presumes the baptism of believers.

From a Scriptural perspective the practice of infant baptism is indefensible. Infant baptism actually arose not from any desire to obey Scripture, but rather from a concern for the salvation of babies and young children who die without an opportunity to respond in baptism to the grace of God. However, from a Baptist perspective, such a concern is misplaced. The eternal welfare of those who die young is not dependent upon whether or not they have submitted to a particular rite of the church. The fact is that God in his love and in his justice will not condemn those who die before the age of discretion, but rather will surely gather all such to himself. To presume that baptism apart from faith can save leads to indulgence in unhelpful superstition.

TO THINK ABOUT . . .

In some Baptist churches in the United States children as young as six years old who profess faith in Jesus are baptised.

What considerations determine the lowest age at which your church will normally baptise believers?

BAPTISM IN AN ECUMENICAL SETTING

ONE BAPTISM

If baptism is for believers only, then how are we to regard those who have been baptised as children? Baptists generally maintain that baptism without faith – whether of children or of adults – is not baptism at all. Baptism without faith has as much validity as a marriage with only one partner present. There is only 'one baptism' – and that is baptism where 'one Lord' is confessed by 'faith' in the waters of baptism (Ephesians 4:4).

In today's ecumenical climate such an approach sounds hard line, not to say intransigent. Some want Baptists to recognise infant baptism as an alternative rite to believers' baptism – pointing out that infant baptism is accompanied by the faith of the godparents, and followed up with faith at the time of confirmation. Most Baptists, however, still have difficulties. They willingly accept their paedobaptist brothers' and sisters' standing in Christ – they cannot, however, accept their practice in this matter.

OPEN MEMBERSHIP

Unlike the vast majority of other Baptist groups, most British Baptists have been prepared to make one concession towards other Christians: their practice of 'open membership'. In many English Baptist churches, it is not necessary to have been baptised as a believer to become a member. This practice, which goes back to the time of John Bunyan, is operated in a number of ways.

Some churches operate open membership on an 'indiscriminate' basis, and accept any unbaptised Christians into membership, whether or not they have been members previously of a particular church.

Most churches will only accept into membership 'unbaptised' Christians (i.e. not baptised as believers) who have already been in good standing with another church and who, for one reason or another, do not feel able in all good conscience to be baptised as believers. The only way to membership for new Christians who have come to faith within those churches is through baptism.

This may seem a strange compromise, but there are in fact theological grounds for this practice. If baptism is a 'rite of initiation', then the baptism of those who have been Christians for a good number of years and who have been in good standing with another Christian church would not really be baptism in the New Testament sense!

BELIEVERS' BAPTISM WITHOUT IMMERSION

A different problem is posed by those who have been baptised as believers, but not by total immersion. Is such baptism without immersion true baptism? How are we to regard those who, for instance, have come to faith within the Anglican church and have been baptised by sprinkling? Although the symbolism of baptism naturally demands immersion, the distinctive aspect of the Baptist approach to baptism is not the quantity of water but rather the quality of faith. If a choice has to be made, then the emphasis must be upon *believers'* baptism rather than on baptism *by immersion*.

This understanding of baptism has allowed many, although not all, Baptists to accept as valid the baptism of those baptised as believers in another church. Indeed, it is an interesting fact of history that the first Baptists made their stand on believers' baptism using affusion and were already seen as Baptists. Immersion was introduced a few years later and was greatly preferred.

TO THINK ABOUT . . .

What is the practice in your church regarding 'open membership'?

What are your views on issues over re-baptism, raised in the previous paragraphs?

BAPTISM AND CHRISTIAN LIFESTYLE

We have already seen that baptism has ethical implications. According to Paul in Romans 6:4, to be baptised is to die to the old and rise to a new way of living. The logic of all this is that Christians may not 'go on sinning' (Rom 6:1–2); for the new life in Christ, witnessed to in the waters of baptism, inevitably entails a new lifestyle.

Baptism is far more than a mere one-off act of obedience; it involves a life-long commitment to the way of Christ. It is desirable, therefore, for prospective baptismal candidates to think through carefully the implications of their baptism. The parables of the Tower Builder and the Warring King (Luke 14: 28–33) are relevant here. Christian discipleship, of which baptism is the sign, is costly. In today's society it means going against the stream. As Jesus himself said, 'If any want to become my followers, let them deny themselves and take up their cross and follow me' (Mark 8:34 NRSV).

In practical terms, baptism involves adopting the ethic of the Sermon on the Mount. It means, for instance, saying no to sex outside marriage (Matt 5:27–30); opting out of the rat-race and putting Christ before your career (Matt 6:24). It means in many respects turning your back on the world and the world's values. To be baptised is to be a non-conformist in the truest sense of the word.

A nonconformist, however, is not an individualist. As we have already seen, baptism involves not only commitment to Christ but also to his people (see 1 Corinthians 12:13). This corporate dimension to baptism also has ethical overtones. It means, for instance, that we may no longer look only to our own interests, but also to the interests of others (Phil 2:4). It means that sharing with God's people who are in need and practising hospitality (Rom 12:13) come to the top of our agenda.

Like marriage, baptism is not to be undertaken 'carelessly, lightly, or selfishly, but reverently, responsibly, and after serious thought'. For baptism involves far more than a momentary confession of the faith – it involves rather a lifetime commitment to the way of Christ, a lifetime commitment to nonconformity. The ethical implications are enormous. In this sense Baptists are radical believers.

TO THINK ABOUT . . .

How in practice can your church keep believers alert to the ethical and lifestyle implications of baptism?

Does it help if you mark annually the anniversary of your baptism and the vows you made?

See later on page 26 for the link between the Lord's Supper and the renewing of baptismal vows.

TO THINK ABOUT . . .

Sally is a mentally handicapped teenager in the local Baptist church who has confessed to love Jesus as her Saviour.

How can the church sensitively and helpfully respond to Sally's request for baptism and church membership?

Four books (*Knowing Jesus, Following Jesus, The Church, Joining the Church*), prepared for people with learning disabilities, are available from The Baptist Union of Great Britain.

'I promise you you'll only be under for a second.'

2

Breaking Bread and Drinking Wine

– Baptists celebrate the Lord's Supper –

CENTRALITY OF THE LORD'S SUPPER

Central to the worship life of the Christian church has been the celebration of the Lord's Supper. On the whole, the church has taken seriously the words of Jesus at the Last Supper: 'This do in remembrance of me.' This was certainly true of the New Testament church.

It is significant that Paul's teaching on the Lord's Supper (1 Cor 11:17–34) is in the context of what takes place when the Corinthians 'come together as a church' (1 Cor 11:18).

Likewise, in Acts 20:7, it would appear that, at Troas at least, the Lord's Supper was celebrated once a week: 'On the first day of the week,' records Luke, 'we came together to break bread.'

Furthermore, Acts 2:46 seems to imply that for the Jerusalem church 'breaking of bread', when presumably the Lord's death was remembered, was a daily occurrence.

Although Baptists happily recognise that the Lord's Supper is an 'ordinance', laid down by the Lord Jesus, in comparison with most other mainline churches, the Lord's Supper is not fully central to most Baptist worship. Although there are exceptions, on the whole the Lord's Supper is not celebrated every Sunday in Baptist churches. Among British Baptists the Lord's Supper is normally held twice a month, and among other Baptist groupings it is even less frequent. Indeed, among some Baptists in the USA the Lord's Supper is celebrated only once a year – on Maundy Thursday.

> **TO THINK ABOUT . . .**
> Is the Lord's Supper 'central' to the worship of your church? Has your church got it right concerning the frequency with which the Lord's Supper is celebrated?
>
> Are there strong arguments for the case that if Baptists wish to treat the Scriptures as normative, then many Baptist churches need to reform their communion practice?

SIGNIFICANCE OF THE LORD'S SUPPER

What precisely do Baptists understand they are doing when they celebrate the Lord's Supper? There is no definitive Baptist statement, but for Baptists the Lord's Supper is a many-sided event.

A MEMORIAL MEAL

Baptists have always viewed the Lord's Supper as a memorial meal. The Lord's Supper, declared the *Particular Baptist Confession* of 1677, is not a

> real sacrifice . . . but only a memorial of that one offering up of himself, by himself, upon the cross, once and for all. (Chapter XXX.)

This approach to the Lord's Supper – often termed 'Zwinglian' after the great Swiss Reformer, Huldreich Zwingli (1484–1531) – is based on the words of Jesus: 'do this in remem-

---

23

brance of me' (1 Cor 11:24–25). In eating the bread and drinking the wine we remember Jesus, and in particular his death. Inevitably this lends a solemn aspect to the Lord's Supper, as we focus on the crucified Saviour of Calvary. For not only do we remember his sufferings, we remember that it was for our sake that 'he hung and suffered there'.

Yet it is precisely this act of remembering which causes us to be thankful. For as we remember our sins, we remember too that 'the blood of Jesus, his Son, purifies us from every sin' (1 John 1:7). To eat the bread and drink the wine is to receive afresh the assurance of the forgiveness of our sins. Here is the glory of the Cross. However much we fail him, however far we fall, in Jesus there is always a new beginning for those who truly and earnestly repent of their sins. Our sorrow is therefore intermingled with joy as we look back and remember the Christ crucified.

AN ENCOUNTER WITH THE RISEN LORD

The Lord's Supper, however, cannot be a *mere* memorial meal, not least because the Saviour who died is also the Lord who rose. As we remember Jesus, we become aware of his presence with us now. To celebrate the Lord's Supper is to receive yet another opportunity to encounter the risen Lord.

Roman Catholics have seen in the consecrated bread and wine the body and blood of Jesus, which has led them to talk of the 'real presence' of Jesus. While Baptists cannot accept this doctrine of transubstantiation, they can affirm that Jesus is 'spiritually' present at the Table. To feed on Jesus by faith (John 6:56–57) is a biblical metaphor expressing the fellowship which Christians may experience with their Lord. Although Jesus may not come nearer to us in the bread and wine, we through eating bread and drinking wine may come nearer to him. Luke tells us that the couple on the Emmaus Road recognised Jesus in the breaking of bread (Luke 24:30–31).

That experience has been repeated in the lives of many Christians since. For what is true of worship in general is true of the Lord's Supper in particular: as we 'draw near to God' we discover ourselves caught up into heaven itself and join with the great multitude around the throne (Heb 10:18–25).

> **TO THINK ABOUT . . .**
>
> John has been a church member for ten years. He admits that he finds it easier to understand the 'memorial meal' aspect of the Lord's Supper than to experience there an 'encounter with the risen Lord'.
>
> Is John typical of Baptists you know? If so, why the strong emphasis on the 'memorial' aspect? How would you help John to see the Supper as much more than an occasion for gratefully remembering?

A TASTE OF HEAVEN

The Lord's Supper also contains a future aspect. For Jesus not only commanded his disciples to remember him in this way 'until he comes' (1 Cor 11:26), he also said that he would drink no more wine 'until that day when I drink it anew with you in my Father's kingdom' (Matt 26:29). Underlying this is the Jewish picture of the Kingdom of God as a great banquet (see, for instance, Isa 25:6). Jesus, as he instituted this Supper, looked forward to the coming of God's kingdom. In turn, as we eat and drink, we too look forward to that day when suffering and death are no more, and when, together with all God's people, we will be united with God himself (Rev 21:3–4). In this sense, the Lord's Supper offers a taste of heaven.

Baptists – along with many other Christians in their 'celebration' of the Lord's Supper – have not always successfully combined this note of triumph with their focus on the Cross. In spite of their antipathy toward a crucifix, many Baptists at the Lord's Supper tend to gaze on the form of the dying Saviour, and miss out on the enthronement of the Lamb (see Rev 5). Indeed, British Baptists traditionally have not talked of 'celebrating' the Lord's Supper, but rather of 'observing the ordinance'. Perhaps not surprisingly, some of these 'observances' have missed the element of joy.

Fortunately, the tide is beginning to turn and many churches end their celebrations of the

'No Godfrey, take out more than that. He said its for the "poor members of the church". We are very poor members; we haven't been here since last Harvest!'

Lord's Supper with a hymn of triumph in which the lordship of the risen and returning Christ is to the fore.

AN EXPRESSION OF FELLOWSHIP

For Baptists the Lord's Supper has always provided an opportunity for expressing personal devotion. As the bread is eaten and the wine drunk, private prayer is encouraged. However, Baptists have never treated the Lord's Supper as a time for individualism, but rather as an occasion for expressing their fellowship in Christ. And rightly so. For as we draw nearer to Christ we draw nearer to one another. According to Paul, the one loaf is a symbol of our oneness in Christ (1 Cor 10:17). The Lord's Supper inevitably has a corporate dimension – after all, its origin was in a meal for a group of friends.

There was a time in Baptist church life when this corporate dimension was emphasised by the taking of a communion offering for the poorer members of the fellowship. In many churches this has fallen into disuse – not least because of the desire to have an 'all-in-budget' which dispenses with a communion offering.

There are, however, other ways in which fellowship can be expressed. In many Baptist churches it is at the Lord's Table that new

members are given the right hand of fellowship and welcomed into membership (see Gal 2:9).

Again, it is customary in many churches to share news of the fellowship at the Lord's Table and to remember the needs of the fellowship in prayer.

Many churches have revived the ancient Christian practice of declaring the Peace, when an opportunity is given for members of the congregation to greet and bless one another (see Rom 16:16; 2 Cor 13:12; 1 Thess 5:26; 1 Pet 5:14).

Where individual communion glasses are used, another way of expressing fellowship is waiting until all are served, before drinking together. In such ways Baptists affirm that the Lord's Supper is a fellowship meal.

> **TO THINK ABOUT . . .**
> **By what other means does or could your church effectively express the fellowship significance of the Lord's Supper?**

AN OPPORTUNITY FOR REDEDICATION

If the Lord's Supper is meaningful, then it will end in renewed dedication – it will spur us onwards in our service of Christ. Indeed, sometimes at the Lord's Table we read the words of the Psalmist:

> How can I repay the Lord for all his goodness to me? I will lift up the cup of salvation and call on the name of the Lord. I will fulfil my vows to the Lord in the presence of all his people'. (Psalm 116:12–14)

Although traditionally Baptists have not used the term 'sacrament' of the Lord's Supper – no doubt reacting against some of the magical associations with the word found in certain church traditions – it is good to be aware that the Latin word 'sacramentum' at one time meant a soldier's oath of loyalty to his emperor. In this sense the Lord's Supper can be sacramental: for, as we gather around the Table and rejoice in the Saviour's power today, we may renew our baptismal vows to the Lord who loved us and gave himself for us.

A TYPICAL BAPTIST CELEBRATION OF THE LORD'S SUPPER

A typical Baptist celebration of the Lord's Supper will include the following elements:

OPENING WORSHIP

The Lord's Supper is part and parcel of the main worship of the church. Twenty or more years ago, most English Baptist churches had a custom of making the Lord's Supper into an optional extra service tagged on to the main service and often attended by only a few. The reason for the separation between the main service and the communion service was to ensure that the table was 'fenced' and that only committed Christians took the bread and wine. However, such a 'fencing' often resulted in Christians regarding the service as an optional extra, rather than as central to the church's worship. Today the vast majority of English Baptist churches have integrated the Lord's Supper into the main worship service.

Although the Lord's Supper belongs primarily to Sunday worship, there seems no good reason to restrict it to one of the main services of worship. There is much to be said, for instance, for a home group celebrating the Lord's Supper.

While their understanding of the priesthood of all believers leads most Baptists to accept that an ordained pastor need not be present at every celebration of the Lord's Supper, nonetheless they tend to feel that purely private celebrations of the Lord's Supper run counter to the spirit of Paul's teaching in 1 Corinthians 11, and so run the risk of bringing the church of God into contempt (see 1 Cor 11:27).

TO THINK ABOUT . . .

What views do you have about someone other than an ordained pastor presiding at the Lord's Supper? Why do you feel and think as you do?

Several options are possible concerning the celebration of the Lord's Supper by a small group, perhaps a house group, within the church.

- The church discourages the practice, believing that it fragments the unity of the body of Christ.
- The group goes ahead without any 'authorisation' from the church or its leadership.
- The group informs and/or seeks the blessing of the church's leadership.
- The group seeks the blessing and support of the church meeting.

Which option do you favour and why?

THE PROCLAMATION OF THE WORD

Just as at the Last Supper a solemn account of the events leading up to the first Passover was recited (see Ex 12:26–27), so when the first Christians gathered to break bread and drink wine, they would have recited the story of how God in Christ had set his people free. This is behind the words of Paul in 1 Corinthians 11:26. It is not the eating and drinking which proclaim, but the actual telling of the story of our salvation. Baptists, with their emphasis on preaching, have traditionally combined the proclamation of the Word with the celebration of the Supper.

In recent years some Baptists have sought to make the Lord's Supper more central to their worship by having communion before the sermon. Others feel unhappy with this practice. They argue that this is a very strange innovation. In the Supper we respond to the love of God. Allowing the Supper to precede the Word, they contend, runs the risk of reducing the eating of bread and drinking of wine to a magical rite; it also distorts the logical flow of the service and causes the sermon to appear very much an optional extra.

A strong case can be made for the Lord's Supper being the climax to all the worship that has gone before. However, the mere fact that the Lord's Supper comes at the end of the service does not guarantee it being the highpoint – it can just as

well be an addendum, if the sermon is not seen to link clearly with the Supper. This does not mean that every sermon at communion needs to centre around the cross. On the other hand, it may mean that every communion sermon says something about the grace of God and our need to respond to it. What a wonderful constraint!

> **TO THINK ABOUT . . .**
> Does the point about the Supper being a response to the Word mean that it is never right for the sermon to follow the Supper, or are there occasions when that order would be appropriate?

GREETING ONE ANOTHER AT THE TABLE

At some stage within any worship service there is much to be said for giving members of the congregation an opportunity to greet one another. Of course, such a greeting is not dependent on the Lord's Supper, but it seems appropriate to offer it then as we remember the one who broke down 'the dividing wall of hostility' and has made us 'one' (Eph 2:14–15).

This time of greeting may be the occasion when those who, for various reasons, have been out of fellowship with one another, reaffirm their

'Mummy, why has Daddy got his fist clenched behind his back?'

relationship in Christ. For only where relationships are right is worship acceptable. In this respect, Jesus' teaching in Matthew 5:23–24 comes to mind:

> Therefore, if you are offering your gift at the altar and there remember that your brother has something against you, leave the gift there in front of the altar. First go and be reconciled to your brother; then come and offer your gift.

Although Jesus is not referring primarily to the Lord's Supper, the underlying principle makes the passage relevant; a precondition for worship is right relationships.

This was a major issue for Paul in his dealings with the church at Corinth. Indeed, he goes so far as to say: 'anyone who eats and drinks without recognising the body of the Lord [i.e. the church] eats and drinks judgment on himself' (1 Cor 11:29). However, ideals are not always practicable. Relationships cannot normally be restored within a matter of minutes. It may be better for a church member to abstain from communion rather than indulge in cheap reconciliation.

THE INVITATION TO THE TABLE

In Baptist history the question of who was or was not invited to the meal has been a matter of controversy. John Smyth, for instance, argued that 'only baptised persons must partake'. John Bunyan, however, felt otherwise. In his *Difference in judgement about water baptism no bar to communion* (1673) he wrote:

> The Church of Christ hath no warrant to keep out of communion the Christian that is discovered to be a visible saint of the word, the Christian that walketh according to his own light.

For the next two centuries 'terms of communion' continued to dominate discussion among Baptists. Today all churches in membership with the Baptist Union of Great Britain have an open table, whereas 'Strict and Particular Baptists' normally close the table to those who have not been baptised as believers.

Many British Baptists have come to invite to the table 'all those who love our Lord Jesus Christ'. But is the invitation now too open? In theory, if

we truly love Jesus, we will want to love his people and commit ourselves to them by becoming church members, but in practice such an invitation results in people who are not members of any church eating bread and drinking wine. Yet if 1 Corinthians 11:27–29 is any guide, then this is surely tantamount to not 'recognising the body of the Lord' and thus eating and drinking 'in an unworthy manner'. The Lord's Supper is surely for the Lord's people, and the Lord's people by definition will be those who have publicly committed themselves to the Lord and his people.

In Baptist terms, this means that ideally the table is open to those who have been baptised as believers and have become members of their local churches. On the other hand, many Baptists are unhappy with this approach and feel that church membership is not a requirement for participation at the Lord's Table. Yet if Baptists are to take their theology seriously, then such a position becomes illogical. For, in a Baptist context, baptism and church membership are the inevitable signs of commitment to the Lord Jesus and his people. It therefore does not make sense theologically, for instance, to allow young people, who have been brought up in a Baptist church, to eat bread and drink wine before they have been baptised and become members of the church.

TO THINK ABOUT . . .

Does the author convince you by his argument? If not, what leads you to a different position?

Should pastoral sensitivity sometimes override matters of principle – for example, in the case of adult members of a congregation who are neither baptised nor church members but who wish to come to the Lord's Table?

Does the author's argument deal satisfactorily with children in the congregation who profess to love Jesus as their Saviour, but who are neither baptised nor church members?

One important exception to this argument, however, needs to be made. In so far as the Lord's Supper is for the Lord's people – and not just for Baptists – in these days of divided understanding on the biblical doctrine of baptism, we cannot restrict the table just to Baptists and others who have been baptised as believers, but rather include all those who are in good standing with their local churches, whatever that implies in each church. In this way, the table is still open – and yet not open indiscriminately.

> **TO THINK ABOUT . . .**
> How would you word the invitation to the Table?

THE 'WORDS OF INSTITUTION'

The 'words of institution' are generally taken from 1 Corinthians 11:23–26, where Paul details the tradition concerning the Lord's Supper which was handed down to him. However, there is no reason why accounts of the Last Supper from the Gospels should not be used too. Almost certainly those accounts owe their places in the Gospels to their usage in celebrations of the Lord's Supper. In addition, Baptists will often include a selection of other appropriate Scriptures which throw light on other aspects of the Lord's Supper (Psa 116:12–14, 17; Isa 53; Matt 5:6; John 3:16; 6:35; 1 Tim 1:15; 1 John 4:9–10).

THE PRAYER(S) OF THANKSGIVING

Baptist churches vary as to whether there is one prayer of thanksgiving for the bread and wine, or two – one for the bread and the other for the wine. On scriptural grounds, two might appear best, since the record says that our Lord gave thanks twice. In fact, if Jesus and his disciples observed the normal Passover routine, there would have been four prayers of thanksgiving! At that Last Supper, however, our Lord gave special significance to the breaking of bread at the beginning of the meal, as also to the drinking of the 'cup of blessing' (which in the context of a Passover Meal was the third cup over which a formal benediction was said). Increasingly

Baptist churches are patterning themselves on the observance of the more liturgical churches and having only one prayer of thanksgiving.

Where most Baptist churches differ from many other churches, however, is that normally this prayer is taken not by the pastor but by one of the deacons. This custom derives from a desire to emphasise that Christians need no priest to consecrate the elements. Historically, at least, this has therefore been a protest prayer! For similar reasons, Baptists generally remain in their seats to receive communion, to emphasise that they have no altar and therefore no separate priests. In theory, by serving one another in their pews, Baptists emphasise the doctrine of the priesthood of all believers.

The following quotation from *Patterns and Prayers for Christian Worship* sums up the significance of the Prayer of Thanksgiving:

> The Prayer of Thanksgiving centres on those mighty acts of God whereby our redemption was accomplished. It is a recalling of the Passion story when our Lord was lifted up in suffering and glory, and a looking forward in hope to the final victory of love. It is an act of thanksgiving for the bread and wine which are symbols of the grace of our Lord Jesus Christ. This prayer calls upon the Holy Spirit, that by his presence in their hearts the people may enter into the meaning of the bread and wine, draw near to the risen Christ, and receive him afresh. It concludes with a fitting response of love, gratitude and re-consecration.

> **TO THINK ABOUT . . .**
> Does it matter who offers the Prayer(s) of Thanksgiving at the Lord's Supper? Why or why not?

THE BREAKING OF BREAD AND THE POURING OF WINE

From the accounts of the Last Supper in the Gospels as also in 1 Corinthians 11, it is clear that Jesus gave particular meaning to his action of breaking the bread: 'This is my body, broken for you', he declared. The action of breaking the bread represented his body given up for us. Sadly British Baptists have tended to reduce the

'There's the single loaf, tiny cubes, wholemeal and white, with a few unleavened wafers; then there's a single chalice, glass cup or aluminium cup, with blackcurrant juice, non-alcoholic wine and alcoholic wine. We've catered for everybody's tastes but I don't think that's quite what was intended in 1 Corinthians 10:17.'

symbolism present in this action with their introduction – on grounds of hygiene! – of small cubes of bread. In some churches, if there is bread to break at all, then it is often a piece of thin-sliced white bread. Many Baptists will be pleased that the symbolism of the one loaf is being restored in an increasing number of churches. This expresses the symbolism of the oneness that we have in Christ (see 1 Cor 10:17).

> ### TO THINK ABOUT . . .
> Betty and Tom feel very uncomfortable when their minister holds the loaf up high and breaks it very deliberately. They say it seems so 'priestly' and un-Baptist.
>
> Have they got a point or do they and other Baptists miss a lot by their objections to symbolic actions and gestures?

To those from other Christian traditions, the Baptist use of small individual cups of grape juice seems most strange. It is important to note that this is a relatively recent custom. Earlier Baptists – and still many Baptists on the Continent of Europe – shared a few large cups and thereby emphasised their fellowship with the Lord and with one another (see 1 Cor 10:16).

A change came about in the late nineteenth and the early twentieth century, when the Free Churches in Britain adopted the temperance cause. This led to the non use of alcoholic wine and the adoption of grape-juice or non-alcoholic 'wine', which in turn made many feel that small cups were more hygienic. The argument here turned on the fact that whereas the alcohol present in wine has a certain 'sterilising' effect, grape juice or its equivalent fails to kill off any germs, hence the use of individual cups. Interestingly, this concern for hygiene was due more to advertisers of small communion cups than to doctors!

In many Baptist churches today the symbolism of the one cup is retained by the presence of a silver chalice on the table – along with the small individual cups. It has become customary for the pastor – or whoever is presiding at the table – to lift up the cup in full view of the congregation, as an action corresponding to the breaking of bread. However, in view of the Lord's own reference to his blood being poured out for the forgiveness of sins, might the symbolism of actually pouring the wine into the cup be more appropriate? Perhaps we should bring back the old flagons used by our Baptist forefathers!

TO THINK ABOUT . . .

Henry dislikes the diced cubes of bread used at communion services in his local Baptist church, whilst Mary has vowed she will not come to the Table if a common loaf alone is introduced.

Jenny finds the use of small glasses mildly ludicrous, whilst Bill, who is anxious about his health, would pass the common cup by if it was adopted.

Their pastor is in despair!

How should the church deal with the dilemma?

What is the practice in your church and is it, in your opinion, the right one?

SERVING ONE ANOTHER

Because Baptists do not regard their pastors as priests, there tends to be a greater variety and freedom in the way in which the bread and wine are distributed. Unlike the practice of (most) Anglican and Roman Catholic churches, Baptists do not normally go forward to receive communion, but rather are served the bread and wine as they sit in their seats. Traditionally deacons have served the members of the congregation, but increasingly – in England at least – members of the congregation are encouraged to serve one another, and as they do so to use such phrases as 'the body of Christ was broken for you', 'the blood of Christ was shed for you'. This is the priesthood of all believers in action.

PRAYING FOR OTHERS

Traditionally in many Baptist churches the eating of bread and drinking of wine is followed by a pastoral prayer, where the sick and elderly are prayed for, and other absent members of the fellowship are remembered.

Increasingly in Baptist churches this time is also used to pray for those who are present at the Table. With James 5:16 in mind and its injunction to 'pray for each other so that you may be healed', an invitation is often given to any who would like special prayer, whether for healing or for some other personal concern, to come to the Table for prayer and the laying-on-of-hands. The pastor together with others, whether deacons or not, take part in this ministry. In times past prayer for healing was a private affair, reserved for members of the congregation 'in extremis'. Today, however, there is the recognition that such prayer may be used to benefit God's people at any time.

The Lord's Supper is an occasion for prayer not only for the needs of the local fellowship, but also for the needs of the wider church. It is an appropriate moment to pray for missionaries and the church of Christ overseas, for the local association and for the area superintendent, for the Baptist colleges and other Christian bodies. Here the horizontal dimension of the Lord's Supper receives expression.

Right as it is to focus especially upon God's people, it behoves us to go on and remember the world for whom Christ died. Just as there are no limits to God's love and concern, so too there should be no limits to the love and concern of his church. In other words, prayers of intercession could meaningfully be part of the Lord's Supper.

God's love and concern include, of course, not only people in the present, but also those in the past. Indeed, those who have died in Christ are very much people in the present. In our Baptist tradition we do not pray for the dead, but we can give thanks afresh for the safekeeping of those who have died in Christ, and look forward to the day when we shall be reunited with them – and with all God's people.

Hopefully, somewhere within these prayers, there will also be an opportunity for those gathered around the Table to renew their commitment to the Lord. If our love for our Lord is at all meaningful, then it must issue in action in the week that lies ahead.

> ### TO THINK ABOUT . . .
>
> Baptists need not reject an awareness of those who have died in Christ. The following lines from the Sursum Corda illustrate this:
>
> > Therefore with angels and archangels,
> > and with all the company of heaven,
> > we proclaim your great and glorious
> >   name . . .
>
> How could more be done at a communion service both to recall thankfully the lives of those who have gone before us and to celebrate the ever growing family of God, which includes the living and the dead?

AN OUTBURST OF PRAISE

Baptists in England and elsewhere are learning to combine the note of celebration with the serious and sombre task of remembering. The cross cannot be isolated from the resurrection, just as the resurrection cannot be isolated from the cross.

In some Baptist churches members of the congregation are encouraged, immediately after receiving the bread and wine, to express their love for Jesus by intermingling short prayers of praise and thanksgiving with simple worship songs. The remembrance of Calvary provides fresh stimulus for praise.

Other churches may prefer simply to surround the eating of bread and drinking of wine with periods of private meditation, which may then lead into prayers for others. But even where such an order of service is followed, the service will almost always climax in a final hymn of praise. The hymn might enable the congregation to sing the praises of the risen, ascended and reigning Lord Jesus. Jesus is Lord – not of the church but of the world, Lord of history, Lord of time, Lord before whom every knee shall bow and every tongue confess. With such praise on their lips the congregation may go on their way, with heads held high, rejoicing.

3

Celebrating the Faith

– a Baptist approach to worship –

DIVERSITY IN WORSHIP

A letter from a certain Hughe and Anne Bromehead describes early Baptist worship in Amsterdam:

We begynne with a prayer, after reade some one or tow chapters of the Bible; gyve the sence thereof and conferr upon the same; that done, we lay aside our bookes and after a solemn prayer made by the first speaker, he propoundeth some text owt of the Scripture and prophesieth out of the same by the space of one hower or three quarters of an hower. After him standeth up a second speaker and prophesieth out of the said text the like tyme and space, sometyme more, sometyme less. After him, the third, the fourth, the fifth etc., as the time will gyve leave. Then the first speaker concludeth with prayer as he began with prayer, wth an exhortation to contribution to the poore, which collection being made is also concluded with prayer. This morning exercise begynes at eight of the clocke and continueth until twelve of the clocke. The like course of exercise is observed in the afternwne from two of the clocke unto five or six of the clocke. Last of all the execution of the government of the Church is handled.

TO THINK ABOUT . . .

Look back at this letter with its *olde-worlde* style and spelling. What is familiar to you and what is unfamiliar compared with your normal experience of a worship service?

What do you detect were central aspects of early Baptist worship?

Your immediate reaction may be to thank God that you were not a Baptist in seventeenth-century Amsterdam! The next reaction is possibly to realise that there is no one Baptist pattern of worship, for down through the centuries Baptists have been in the process of change and evolution. Furthermore, what may be acceptable amongst Baptists in one country may not be acceptable in another. Our Russian Baptist brothers and sisters, for instance, are very happy in one service to listen to three sermons, one after the other, so their services are longer than most British Baptists would cope with on a regular basis. But who is to say that one form of service is more Baptist than another?

Baptists are true Nonconformists and as such cherish their liturgical freedom. Unlike Anglicans, they do not have a *Book of Common Prayer* which regulates their orders of service. Although Baptists may produce books of orders and prayers, at the end of the day none of these books are normative. As radical believers, for them the Bible alone is authoritative. Baptists are therefore free – free to respond to the leading of the Spirit, free to respond to the changing circumstances in which they live. In a way which is not always true of some of the more liturgical churches, Baptists – in principle at least – have an enviable flexibility. True, Baptists have not always taken advantage of their liturgical freedom. Indeed, they have at times become as hidebound to tradition as other groups of Christians. But where Baptists are true to their radical roots, there they have freedom to change and vary their patterns of worship.

Yet, for all the diversity of Baptist worship, there is, on the whole, a distinctive Baptist approach to worship. However much Baptist worship may vary, generally speaking there are certain common characteristics.

LET GOD SPEAK

The first general characteristic of Baptist worship is the emphasis on the sermon. Preaching is central to any Baptist worship service. It would be unusual for a Baptist service not to contain a sermon. Furthermore, while in some church traditions eight to ten minutes is deemed quite sufficient, most Baptists feel short-changed with anything under fifteen minutes, and normally expect something in the region of twenty to twenty-five minutes. Indeed, in some Baptist churches, the sermon lasts considerably longer.

'It's a Baptist preaching, so I've brought emergency rations.'

> **TO THINK ABOUT . . .**
> How far has preaching been central in your experience of Baptist worship? Is it central enough in your church?

Because the sermon is the centre-piece of most Baptist worship services, when a church in Britain is looking for a new pastor, the candidate is normally invited to come and 'preach with a view'. It is by their preaching that Baptist pastors generally stand or fall. Not surprisingly, therefore, the training of preachers is a high priority in our Baptist theological colleges.

If a 'sacrament' is a means of God blessing his people, then for Baptists preaching is their primary 'sacrament'. Traditional Baptist church architecture reflects the centrality of the Word by putting the pulpit in a central position, in contrast to the typical Anglican church, where the altar is central and the pulpit is often at the side. Furthermore, Anglican churches almost always have a central aisle, but many Baptist churches have their pews in the centre – even this seating arrangement emphasises that people have come to listen to the Word of God rather than go forward for communion. Today, however, Baptist architecture is in a state of flux. In England there are Baptist churches who are getting rid of their pulpits, preferring a more informal approach to the delivery of the sermon.

> **TO THINK ABOUT . . .**
> Winston, who's a bit of a wag, turned to Jane as they came out of the evening service after a forty minute sermon and said:
>
> 'A person with something to say can say it in twenty minutes – a person with nothing to say needs at least forty.'
>
> Jane replied:
>
> 'That's not fair. Any impatience with long sermons shows people have lost their appetite for Bible teaching.'
>
> Where does your sympathy lie? Should methods of teaching and learning, other than traditional preaching, be used more widely in Baptist churches and if so, what methods?

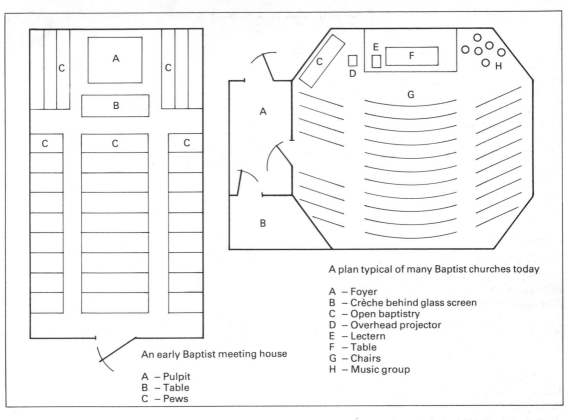

A plan typical of many Baptist churches today

A – Foyer
B – Crèche behind glass screen
C – Open baptistry
D – Overhead projector
E – Lectern
F – Table
G – Chairs
H – Music group

An early Baptist meeting house

A – Pulpit
B – Table
C – Pews

Despite their emphasis on the sermon, Baptists have not always paid great attention to the reading of the Scriptures themselves. Whereas in any given service of worship in the more liturgical churches there are often three Scripture readings (from the Old Testament, the Epistles, and the Gospels), in addition to a Psalm or two, in many Baptist churches today there is only one Scripture reading, and sometimes short at that. Many argue that this practice does not take Scripture seriously enough, and that although God may speak through the sermon, in the first place he speaks through his Word.

> **TO THINK ABOUT . . .**
> **What practice do you think adequately does justice to Paul's advice to Timothy: 'devote yourself to the public reading of Scripture' (1 Tim. 4:13).**
>
> **Who should and who should not read the Bible passages in a service of worship?**

PSALMS, HYMNS AND SPIRITUAL SONGS

EARLY CHURCH

Hymns and songs characterised the life of the early church. Thus the Apostle Paul wrote to the Ephesians: 'Speak to one another with psalms, hymns and spiritual songs. Sing and make music in your heart to the Lord' (Eph 5:19). In similar fashion he wrote to the Colossians:

> Let the word of Christ dwell in you richly as you teach and admonish one another with all wisdom, and as you sing psalms, hymns and spiritual songs with gratitude in your hearts to God (Col 3:16).

It is highly likely that in such passages as Philippians 2:6–11, Colossians 1:15–20 and 1 Timothy 3:16, we have examples of early Christian hymns quoted by the apostle Paul.

BENJAMIN KEACH'S INFLUENCE

Although the example of early Baptist worship at the beginning of this chapter indicates that the first Baptists seem not to have obeyed Paul's injunction, it was not long before Baptists began to make melody to the Lord. Initially there was solo Psalm singing, but then in the late seventeenth century Benjamin Keach (1640–1704), a Baptist pastor, became the first person to introduce hymn singing into an English congregation of any denomination. The significant innovation was to use non-biblical words (though heavily dependent on the Bible) and to have *all* the people singing.

Not surprisingly, this move was not accomplished without controversy. Thirteen of his members transferred their membership in protest. A book was published denouncing this new-fangled practice as worse than infant baptism, and maintaining that it was artificial and therefore alien to the free motions of the Spirit of God! The criticism might have been better directed if the focus had been on the poor quality of Keach's hymns. For example:

> Our wounds do stink and are corrupt,
> Hard swellings we do see;
> We want a little ointment, Lord,
> Let us more humble be.
>
> Here meets them now that worm that gnaws,
> And plucks their bowels out;
> The pit, too, on them shuts her jaws,
> This dreadful is, no doubt.

Keach, however, eventually won the day, and hymn-singing became a feature of Baptist life. In 1769 two Baptists, John Ash and Caleb Evans, published *A Collection of hymns adapted to public worship*, which was in fact the first compilation in England of hymns by different authors. It should be noted, however, that the sixteenth-century Anabaptists were into composing and singing their own hymns and songs long before Benjamin Keach. These hymns were collected in the Anabaptist *Ausbund*, and a translation of one of their hymns, 'Our Father God, thy name we

praise', is included in *Baptist Praise and Worship*.

> **TO THINK ABOUT . . .**
> Suggest some areas of church life today where, like Benjamin Keach, Baptists could be innovative, take risks and engage in imaginative, albeit controversial initiatives.

OLD HYMNS – NEW SONGS

Today Baptists in many parts of the world face a new controversy, where the issue relates to the traditional hymns of the church: are they now so much a feature of the past that only the new songs born of charismatic renewal are acceptable? Is there room for a hymnbook at all in today's church? The British Baptist Psalms and Hymns Trust believed there was and in 1991 published the new hymnbook mentioned above, *Baptist Praise and Worship*. This hymnbook includes not only the great traditional hymns but also some of the more established songs associated with charismatic renewal.

In Britain at least it would now be inconceivable for a Baptist hymnbook not to contain such songs. Here we see that the worship life of the church cannot stand still. Words that seemed fitting to one generation do not always prove acceptable to the next – like the hymns of Benjamin Keach. On the other hand, suitably adapted and modernised, many of the great hymns of the church still express meaningfully the worship of God's people.

A further point needs to be made. In the past Baptists confessed their faith in the singing of their hymns. Although the Apostles Creed and the Nicene Creed are not the exclusive preserve of the historic state churches, Baptists by and large have not used the creeds in worship. Historically this was partly because, in certain of their phrases, creeds used other than biblical language, and partly because subscription to creeds was used in England as a test of office. (i.e. certain positions in public life were barred to you unless you subscribed to the creeds.)

If Baptists were simply to do away with the traditional hymns, they would be robbing themselves, therefore, of an opportunity to confess their faith. For, although generalisations are dangerous, many of the traditional hymns of the church have substance in a way which is not true of many modern worship songs: many of the latter are relatively short and intended for use in a repetitive – if not meditative – fashion. Modern worship songs can be credal in style – indeed a number are – but the use to which they are put tends to be different from that of the hymns.

Many Baptists would argue, therefore, that wise worship leaders in today's churches will emulate the converted scribe and bring out of the church's 'store-room' of praise 'new treasures as well as old' (Matt 13:52). As Paul realised (Eph 5:19 and Col 3:16), variety is an important key to worship: the 'hymns, songs, and psalms' should be varied in content and style to suit the differing tastes and moods of the people of God.

> **TO THINK ABOUT . . .**
>
> How helpfully or unhelpfully are 'psalms, hymns and spiritual songs' used in your church?
>
> Do the Baptist churches you know reflect musically and in other ways the diversity within our culture? Think of some examples of how this does or could happen in your church.

CHOIRS

Another area of controversy relates to the use of church choirs. In most parts of the world a Baptist worship service without a choir is unthinkable. Indeed, singing in the choir is seen by many Baptists outside Britain as an important form of Christian service. In most Baptist

'The sopranos and altos will sing "Glory", the tenors will sing "Hallelujah", and the basses will click their fingers and sing "Doo-doo, da, doo-da-doo".'

churches in Britain, however, church choirs have been disbanded. In their place is the 'music group' with guitars, drums, and other musical instruments. Some choirs have only themselves to blame for their demise. A group of enthusiastic but untutored people, aspiring unsuccessfully to compete with the choir of King's College, Cambridge, will never commend themselves.

But some of the objections raised against choirs are not as strong as they seem. Opinion concerning choirs differs among Baptists and you need to weigh the arguments:

- A choir segregates the congregation.
  No! Having a choir involves differentiation. Don't we believe in a variety of gifts?
- A choir can easily become pure entertainment.
  Yes! Some choirs do seek simply to entertain – but then so do some preachers!
- All those anthems mean little variety in worship.
  Yes, some choirs do get stuck in a groove – just like some preachers who never get their noses out of the epistles. A balanced diet is surely necessary – a choir should be prepared to sing songs coming from charismatic renewal as well as Bach chorales.
- A choir creates a passive congregation.
  That is not much of an argument – a preacher does so even more! But seriously, is listening to be equated with passivity?

Clearly there are a number of issues here. At the end of the day the deciding factor as to whether or not a church has a choir relates more to culture than to theology.

> **TO THINK ABOUT . . .**
>
> There is a growing tendency in Baptist churches towards 'occasional' choirs, who practise specifically for one event or festival and then disband. This avoids, some argue, the danger of 'permanency' which can lead to problems.
>
> How effective do you think a choir, either permanent or occasional, could be in the worship and mission of your church?
>
> How more or less effective is a music group?

MUSIC GROUPS

There was a stage when small orchestras were common place in Baptist churches. Gradually, however, the organ came to dominate the scene and the use of other musical instruments fell away.

Today, however, there is an upsurge in music-making. Many Baptist churches have enthusiastic music groups (often termed 'worship groups'), comprising guitars, synthesizers and drums, with possibly a wide variety of other

'Quite honestly, I haven't thought too much about the theology *of the song. I reckoned that could wait till we got the* notes *right.'*

instruments. In some churches such groups have replaced the organ, in other churches they simply complement the traditional music of the church. It is certainly true that the organ is not always suited to accompany the singing of some of the modern worship songs.

Needless to say, the introduction of such instruments – the drums in particular – has been a matter of some controversy. But then the Scriptures appear to encourage noisy praise. In the words of the Psalmist,

> Praise [God] with the sounding of the trumpet,
> praise him with the harp and lyre,
> praise him with tambourine and dancing,
> praise him with strings and flute,
> praise him with the clash of cymbals,
> praise him with resounding cymbals.
>
> Psalm 150:3–5

The truth is that God does not confine himself to any one particular worship style. As in all things, balance together with a certain 'give and take' is required.

TO THINK ABOUT . . .

Kath and Helen were having coffee together the day after the church meeting decided to begin holding two Sunday morning services – one for those who wanted a 'traditional' service and another for those who wanted a service which was 'lively', with lots of worship songs and congregational participation.

Helen thought it was a great idea because people could choose which suited them. Kath disagreed. She thought it would divide the church and that they ought to hold one service and somehow find a way of meeting everybody's tastes.

Did the church make a wise decision? What contribution would you make to Kath and Helen's conversation?

FREEDOM IN PRAYER

In contrast with the set prayers of the Anglican and Roman Catholic churches, Baptists have traditionally used free forms of prayer. Not for them the Prayer Book. From their beginnings Baptists along with the other Free Churches have been proud of their freedom to address God in whatever manner they deem fit.

ADVANTAGES

The advantages of free prayer are clear.

a. Spontaneity

Free prayers have a greater feel of spontaneity about them. The very form of extempore prayer is warm and direct, intimate and personal, and thereby expresses something of the believers' relationship with God.

b. Relevance

Free prayer is very relevant to the needs of the congregation and of the wider world. By its very nature free prayer can be both immediate and particular.

c. Realism

Free prayer has a greater feeling of reality about it. It is more immediately perceived as a conversation with God. The focus is God – not initially the printed page.

DISADVANTAGES

There are also disadvantages connected with free prayer.

a. Dependent on leader's mood

The congregation can be at the mercy of the worship leader's moods, which may well vary according to weather, health, or general feelings.

b. Stereotyped language

Where free prayer is the order of the day, the language of the one who leads in prayer can become stereotyped, repeating well-worn phrases and pious cliches.

' . . . and I really just ask you, Lord, just to really help me to just really stop saying really and just.'

c. Undisciplined

Free prayer can be wordy, meandering, long and tedious. Bernard Manning, who as a Congregationalist shared a common tradition of prayer with Baptists, once wrote:

> I still feel something of the horror with which the Long Prayer always affected me when I was a boy. Everywhere it was always the same. There appeared to be no chance it would ever end. You simply resigned yourself. Time after time occurred places at which an admirable ending could have been made; but no, 'Pray without ceasing': that apostolic word had been only too carefully observed. I watched the sunbeam broken in windows and caught in the gilt of the hymn book covers; I played every game and then, at last, it was over: and we raised our heads, it seemed to me, like people coming out of our huts after a tornado, anxious to see who is still there and who is missing.

PREPARED FREE PRAYER

No Baptist can fail to recognise the disadvantages of free prayer. We have all suffered at one time or another from prayers that have not been carefully thought out. But that is in fact the key. Free prayer is not necessarily 'extempore' prayer. Isaac Watts, for instance, distinguished between 'conceived' or prepared free prayer, 'done by some work of meditation before we begin to speak in prayer', and 'extempore' free prayer, 'when we without any reflection or meditation before hand address ourselves to God and speak the thoughts of our hearts as fast as we conceive them'.

While extempore free prayer may be right in the home and in prayer meetings, there is much to be said for the prepared free prayer in public services of worship. Indeed, to be fair, that is the way in which many Baptist pastors and worship leaders operate. Would that all did! The fact is that we are free to produce the very best prayers – but we are also free to abuse our freedom and end up with the third-rate.

TO THINK ABOUT . . .

Recall occasions when you were led in bad and unhelpful 'free prayer'. Why did it leave you so dissatisfied?

Does the author's argument for 'prepared free prayer' win your support?

OPEN PRAYER

So far the emphasis has been on the prayer of the worship leader. But in many Baptist churches opportunities are given for worshippers to participate in open prayer within the main Sunday worship services. These opportunities may vary: sometimes there will be a time of 'open worship' where the emphasis is on praise; sometimes spontaneous prayers of intercession may be invited; at other times prayer will be made in response to what God has been saying through the sermon; or gathered around the Lord's Table worshippers may respond with short prayers of adoration or thanksgiving for God's grace in Christ. Prayer, for Baptists, is certainly no 'priestly' monopoly.

TO THINK ABOUT . . .

Does the introduction of open prayer into Baptist worship make a helpful statement against a 'priestly' monopoly of offering prayer, or is the price often paid, for example, inaudibility and undue length, a price too high?

FREEDOM IN WORSHIP

CONGREGATIONAL PARTICIPATION

Baptists not only have freedom in prayer but also in worship generally.

Under the influence of charismatic renewal in particular, congregational participation has been increasingly encouraged in many churches. Along with opportunities for open prayer, other contributions may be invited from the congregation, for example, a word of testimony or a word of encouragement, a reading or a song (see 1 Cor 14:26).

Controversy has raged over the validity of some of the more specific 'charismatic' gifts such as tongues and prophecy. Although, in England at least, most Baptists are willing to acknowledge that in principle the Lord has not withdrawn such gifts, on the whole Baptist churches prefer to follow the apostle Paul's preference and reserve 'tongues' for private use (see 1 Cor 14). As for 'prophecy', that gift along with words of 'wisdom' and 'knowledge' may best be shared in the context of the church meeting, where there is normally better opportunity to 'test' and 'weigh' messages that claim to come from the Lord (see 1 Cor 14:29; 1 John 4:1).

DECENTLY AND IN ORDER

Freedom in worship encompasses not just the more charismatic expressions of Baptist life, but Baptist life in general. There is, for instance, no one Baptist form of worship service. On the other hand, our freedom is not an excuse for disorder. The words of Paul in 1 Corinthians 14:40 should be taken seriously: 'But everything should be done in a fitting and orderly way.'

The introduction to a new Baptist manual, *Patterns and Prayers for Christian Worship* (pp 8–9), makes the following helpful comment on 1 Corinthians 14:40:

> The Greek word translated 'decently' is also the origin of the word 'scheme'. It conveys the idea of things coordinated to a common purpose and

points to a pattern which has its own inner logic. Early in the chapter Paul writes, 'For God is not a God of disorder but of peace' (v33), and in Genesis we are told that the Spirit of God moved upon the waters (Gen 1:2) bringing order out of chaos. This is more than a statement about how the world was begun: it is a claim that this is how the world always is, held in orderly existence by God's Spirit which pervades all things. Yet the Spirit is not a creator of stereotypes. It is the unexpected that occurs within the basic pattern that is stimulating and exciting. Though all roses are the same, no two are identical. The elusive quality we call beauty is seen in the variations that give liveliness and interest. Worship too should have an underlying order that is not a chain but an invitation to freedom.

However free or open worship is, there always needs to be some kind of structure in which the various ingredients basic to worship are found. It has often been said that the essential ingredients of Spirit-inspired worship find their roots in the Jewish synagogue and the Upper Room. To the *praise* and *prayer*, the *Scripture readings* and the *sermon* – all characteristics of the Jewish synagogue – were added the *breaking of bread* and the *fellowship* of the Upper Room.

All these six ingredients need to find expression in the worship of our churches today, however the service is ordered. Indeed, it may be that in this particular area of Baptist life, other churches could help us reform ourselves.

TO THINK ABOUT . . .

Recognising that there is no one God-given way of ordering worship, how would you structure a service so that worship flows in a logical and balanced manner?

How would you ensure that everyone participated in the worship?

Set down one or two orders of service as examples of your thinking.

AIDS TO WORSHIP

HISTORICAL CAUTION

British Baptists have traditionally been very suspicious of any physical aids to worship, with the result that it was well into the second half of this century before even simple wooden crosses were displayed in the average British Baptist church. Baptist worship has been very much a cerebral exercise. The preaching of the Word has been at the centre of worship, with the result that people's response to God has been stimulated primarily by words. In the past, at least, there was little attempt to evoke worship through other means.

This approach to worship received expression in Baptist architecture. The early Baptist 'meeting houses', as the first Baptist church buildings were called, were plain in the extreme. They were not adorned with symbols of the Christian faith or stained glass windows that depicted Biblical scenes. For Baptists the church has been first and foremost the people of God, and not the building. Hence in Wales and elsewhere, many Baptists – along with other Nonconformists – have preferred to speak of their buildings as 'chapels' rather than as 'churches'. Biblically speaking, of course, such an emphasis is entirely right. Paul, for instance, wrote to the church at Corinth: 'we are the temple of the living God' (2 Cor 6:16), a statement which implies that God dwells wherever his people are found, and not in any particular building. This same thought is reflected in the words of Jesus: 'where two or three come together in my name, there am I with them' (Matt 18:20). Church buildings are indeed secondary.

MODERN TRENDS

The fact that church buildings are secondary does not mean, however, that such buildings need be plain in the extreme. Church architecture can be both an expression of worship and a vehicle of worship. British Baptists have come to accept that the way a building is constructed and decorated can be helpful to worship. The use of Christian symbols of various kinds has therefore become increasingly common in British Baptist churches. Stained glass windows of modern design and crosses of various shapes and sizes are now much more the norm. Many churches, too, will happily decorate their walls with bright banners, which not only give expression to various aspects of the Christian faith, but are seen also as helpful aids for worship.

In spite of this more positive approach to aids to worship, there is still a certain reserve in this area amongst British Baptists. Apart from the Advent wreath with its four candles (and that is a relatively new custom), few British Baptist churches would follow their sister Scandinavian Baptist churches and have lighted candles on their communion tables – for the older generation at least, that would smack too much of 'papism'. In some churches 'liturgical' dancing is encouraged as an expression of and aid to worship – on the other hand, there are those who are highly suspicious of such a display of the (normally) female form!

TO THINK ABOUT . . .

Are you helped in worship by the architecture of your church building? If not, why?

How would you set about 'improving' it? What 'aids to worship' would you introduce into the building and why?

What features of the plan of a modern Baptist church on page 35 would help you in worship? How would you 'improve' on the lay-out?

MAKING THE MOST OF THE CHRISTIAN YEAR

As part of their Nonconformity Baptists have been very suspicious of the Christian Year. Traditionally the observance of special days has been frowned upon, and texts such as Galatians 4:10 and Colossians 2:16 have been cited in support of their non-observance.

However, in Britain and elsewhere many Baptist churches now recognise that their worship can be enriched through an imaginative celebration of a simplified liturgical year. Celebrating the Christian festivals of Christmas, Easter and Pentecost, as also marking the seasons of Advent and Lent (including Maundy Thursday and Good Friday), does add richness and colour to worship. Furthermore, whatever the preferences of the preacher, it ensures that in worship the congregation has a regular opportunity to focus upon the main events in the life of Jesus.

In addition to celebrating the main Christian festivals, many Baptist churches also mark such events as the end of the year and the beginning of another with Watchnight services and Covenant services; town churches as well as country churches celebrate Harvest Festival, often with special offerings for the poor in the two-thirds world; and, of course, there is the Church Anniversary and in some churches even the Sunday School Anniversary, all of which call for special preaching.

There are also many other special days which churches may observe. Every year the Baptist World Alliance invites Baptists to mark the first Sunday in February as Baptist World Alliance Day. The last two Sundays of January normally mark the beginning and end of the Week of Prayer for Christian Unity. Then there is Mothering Sunday and Fathers' Day. The list is endless. Clearly churches need to be discerning, for not every Sunday can be 'special'. Nor must churches ever forget that first and foremost it is the resurrection of Jesus which they celebrate on the first day of the week.

'Next Sunday we celebrate with special services the first anniversary of our campaign to ban all special Sundays.'

TO THINK ABOUT . . .

Baptists have been influenced in the twentieth century by both the Liturgical Movement (an emphasis on form and structure in worship, with a strong commitment to observing the Christian Year) and the Charismatic Movement (an emphasis on freedom in worship, congregational participation, exercise of spiritual gifts and a note of triumph and celebration).

Are these emphases in opposition to each other? If not, how in practice can Baptists fruitfully merge these two streams of influence?

THE DEDICATION SERVICE

Within any family the birth of a child is a major event and a cause for celebration. For Christian parents it seems natural and right to share their joy with the wider family of the church, publicly giving thanks to God for the gift of their new child and seeking God's blessing on this new life.

And yet what seems natural and right has been treated by many Baptists in the world with grave suspicion. For example, most Baptists in the USA and not a few Baptists on the Continent of Europe believe that to hold a service where a child is at the centre of attention inevitably leads to confusion with infant baptism and so reject the whole idea.

British Baptists, however, have been willing to take the 'risk', and increasingly since the latter part of the nineteenth century have tended to hold 'dedication services'.

TO THINK ABOUT . . .

Is 'Dedication Service' the best title for this occasion?

The Baptist worship manual, *Patterns and Prayers for Christian Worship*, prefers the term 'Infant Presentation'. A leaflet produced by the Baptist Union in the 'Baptist Basics Series' has the title: *The blessing of infants and the dedication of parents*.

Which term to describe the service would you argue for and why?

BIBLICAL GROUNDS

Baptists being Baptists, they have often tried to give biblical justification for this practice. Some point to the story of Samuel's dedication in 1 Samuel 1:27–28. However, the parallel with a twentieth-century dedication service is scarcely exact, for nobody ever hands over their child to the Lord in the way that Hannah handed over her child. Others refer to the presentation of Jesus in the Temple (Luke 2:22), but again the parallel is not appropriate: sacrifices are not generally held at dedication services! What is more, this ceremony only applied to the first-born, the child who was considered to belong to the Lord and had to be 'redeemed' by him.

The most helpful parallel is found in the story of Jesus blessing the children (Matt 19:13–15; Mark 10:13–16; Luke 18:15–17), yet even there the parallel is not exact: the occasion seems only to have been one of blessing, with no act of dedication on the parents' part.

Honesty compels us to admit that there are no biblical grounds as such for this custom. But there are no biblical grounds as such for weddings and funerals being held in a church. However, just as it seems to us right and proper to mark weddings and funerals with a Christian service, so it is equally right and proper to mark the birth of a child in the same way. It is natural to want to thank God for the gift of a child and to ask his blessing on that child. Furthermore, the birth of a child is of such importance that it demands the utmost parents can give, as it also calls for the utmost grace that God can give. In other words, a 'dedication service' is primarily a service of thanksgiving for and blessing of the child, and in which the parents dedicate themselves to their responsibility.

THE CHURCH'S ROLE

It is important to note that the church has a role on such an occasion. In churches that practise infant baptism, there are always godparents, who promise to help the child concerned 'to live and grow in the Christian faith' (*Alternative Service Book*). At a service of dedication in a Baptist church godparents are not present, instead the church promises its support for the child in question. Thus in one order of service the church is addressed:

> As a congregation we too are involved in the Christian upbringing of . . . In our life together we are called to set an example of love and service. However, in particular I would ask the members of this church to befriend, encourage and pray for this family, so that . . . may in due time come to trust Christ as Saviour and confess him as Lord in baptism. If you, the members of this church are so willing, will you signify your acceptance by saying, 'We do'.

Church members, in responding positively to such a question, express their commitment to one another, which – as we have already seen – is of the essence of church membership. In a large church, alas, it is easy for this expression of commitment to have little meaning. All the more need, therefore, for larger churches to find meaningful ways and means of supporting families.

Traditionally Baptists express their support for families by organising all kinds of weekly activities for children and young people. But important as such activities are, they do not meet every need. If a church is to take its commitment to families seriously, then children's 'ministries' need to be developed which are firstly people-centred, rather than activity-centred. There are times when children's most pressing needs are not to be busily occupied, but to be allowed to talk and express whatever is on their hearts.

TO THINK ABOUT . . .

How in practice can your church fulfil its responsibilities to the children within its life and community?

Suggest some examples of 'people-centred ministries'.

Ken stood up at a church meeting when this theme was on the agenda and suggested that they might adopt the practice of having 'sponsors' or 'godparents' who promised to offer practical and prayerful support for children brought to an Infant Presentation Service. The suggestion created lively discussion.

What do you think of the idea?

AN EVANGELISTIC OPPORTUNITY

Baptists tend to regard the dedication service as an 'in-house' affair – the guest list is normally limited to the grandparents and other relatives.

However, from an evangelistic perspective, there is much to be said for exploiting what many people outside our churches often regard as a form of dry baptism. What a difference it would make, for instance, if the new parents invited not only their parents and relatives, but also their neighbours, their colleagues at work, their acquaintances in general. Who could fail to turn down an invitation couched along these lines: 'We're having a special service for our new baby. Do come along and join us. What's more, after the service there'll be a lunch party at home.' It would be churlish to refuse – not least in view of the party to follow! The upshot could be that the congregation is swelled by thirty or more guests, many of whom perhaps do not normally darken the doors of a church. Handled with sensitivity, this could be a great occasion for preaching the gospel.

So far the assumption has been that a dedication service is for Christian families alone – and certainly most requests for such a service come from church families. But what about non-believers who wish to bring their child for a dedication service? Provided the parents are genuinely wanting to take God seriously – as distinct, for instance, from wanting to please one set or other of their parents by having the child 'done' – there seems no good reason to refuse. A parallel can be drawn with the marriage service, which too is open to Christians and non-Christians alike. Dedication, like marriage, belongs in the first place to the order of creation rather than the order of redemption. The service may not have the same meaning as for a Christian, but nonetheless it could still have some meaning.

TO THINK ABOUT . . .

What is your church's practice with regard to a Dedication/Infant Presentation Service involving non-believing parents?

Why has the church adopted that policy?

CHILDREN AND THE CHURCH

The fact that Baptists do not baptise children does not mean that children have no place in the life of a Baptist church. Far from it; the average Baptist church normally has a wide range of activities catering for children of all ages.

CHILDREN IN WORSHIP

Within the worshipping life of Baptist churches there is often a brief spot when children become central to the service. Although the advent of morning Sunday School has removed the justification for the old-fashioned 'children's address', with its three points and its complicated visual aids, many churches still ensure that one part of the morning service is specifically related to the needs of the children.

Unfortunately there has sometimes been a temptation to downgrade the worship at this particular point. There is something to be said for exposing children to the normal worship of the church and thereby allowing them to experience a sense of God's presence amongst his people. Children need, for example, to become familiar with the great hymns of the church, as well as to sing the newer worship songs.

Theologically Baptists have always seen children being within the scope of Christ's saving work. Thus with regard to the fate of those who die in childhood, which for some paedobaptists has been an additional reason for practising infant baptism, Baptists believe that children, who neither sin with impunity nor consciously reject

'So, remember children, next time you see a clown juggling on a unicycle and blowing up balloons, that Gideon trusted in God and slew the Midianites.'

the word of God in Christ, are included in the solidarity of the redeemed with Christ (see Rom 5:12–21; 2 Cor 5:14–15). As for children of Christian parents, Baptists view their position as analagous to those who in earlier times were being prepared for baptism and full membership of the church (catechumens): i.e. children of believers are within the church, not outside it, but their entry into full membership awaits their confession of Christ in baptism.

TO THINK ABOUT . . .

The charter 'Children and the Church', published by the Baptist Union Mission Office, states: 'The full diet of Christian worship is for children as well as adults.'

How much of that 'full diet' are the children in your church involved in? How much should they be involved in?

CHILDREN AND BAPTISM

It is, however, a matter of debate amongst Baptists whether or not older children may be baptised. No Baptist questions the need for baptismal candidates to be believers. The question rather centres around the stage at which a person can make a meaningful commitment to Jesus Christ. Is a simple 'decision' to follow Jesus sufficient? Many Baptists in the USA believe it is, and as a result it is not uncommon for children as young as six or seven to be baptised. In Europe, and in many other parts of the world, baptising children so young would be unthinkable.

Many argue that it is not sufficient for a prospective baptismal candidate to love Jesus as Saviour – rather they must be able to own him as Lord. Furthermore, owning Jesus as Lord, they contend, should involve some understanding of Mark 8:34 (as distinct from simply John 3:16), for the call to discipleship is a costly call to the way of the cross. Such an understanding is surely well-nigh impossible for a child, and implies that normally mid-adolescence is the earliest period when baptism might be meaningful. If conversion is perceived as a process, then the fact that baptism may be delayed until teenage years does not necessarily deny the validity of any earlier experience of Christ.

TO THINK ABOUT . . .

Someone has likened baptism to marriage and argued that, since both involve making public vows and binding yourself to another in faithfulness for life, 'youthful desire and enthusiasm are not enough to qualify for baptism'.

What do you think and why?

CHILDREN AND CHURCH MEMBERSHIP

Needless to say, once a person is deemed eligible, in terms of being old enough, for baptism, that moment too they are eligible for church membership. There are no theological grounds for the custom found in a few Baptist churches of imposing a minimum age for church membership, even though there may be no minimum age for baptism. This does not necessarily mean that every 'child' or young person has to be given voting rights at a church meeting. As we shall argue later, to be able to vote at a church meeting is far from the essence of church membership.

Whether or not children or young people are formally members of the church, the Baptist theology of children hopefully implies a commitment on the part of the church to care for all the children in its charge. There is an increasing recognition amongst Baptists that children are individuals in their own right, and are therefore as much in need of pastoral care as older people in the church. Thus, for instance, in times when a family suffers from the effects of divorce, death or redundancy, children need as much support as their parents. Interestingly amongst New Zealand Baptists 'ministers of children' are emerging, whose task it is to care for the children of the church.

CHILDREN AND THE LORD'S SUPPER

One practical consequence arising from the Baptist theology of baptism is that children do not generally participate in the Lord's Supper. Children may certainly be present at such a service, but until they have fully committed themselves to Christ and his church through baptism and church membership, they may not share in the bread and the wine. Amongst a small minority of Baptists, however, there is a move to follow recent practice amongst some Anglicans by encouraging the participation of children and allowing them to receive the bread. In theory for Anglicans this may make sense, because at least such children have been 'baptised' as infants. However, many Baptists regard such a practice as unacceptable. The Lord's Table, they argue, is for the Lord's people, and within the context of a Baptist church the Table is open in the first place only to those who have committed themselves to the Lord and his people in the waters of baptism. Children need to be recognised, but this is not the most helpful way of giving recognition.

TO THINK ABOUT . . .

Claire, who is nine, had hardly got into the car after the morning service before she poured out to Mum and Dad her sense of injustice.

'Although I'm a Christian, the deacon didn't offer me the bread and wine. Why not,' she asked, 'it's not fair!'

How would you have responded to Claire?

What are some helpful ways of 'recognising' children at the Lord's Table?

4

Living together in Community

– a Baptist understanding of church membership –

At the heart of Baptist faith lies our doctrine of the church. Indeed, it is a radical concept of the church, rather than a particular view of baptism, which is central for Baptists. To put it another way, the Baptist doctrine of believers' baptism stems from the Baptist doctrine of a believers' church.

For Baptists the church is a community of believers gathered together out of the world, who have committed themselves to Christ and to one another. Traditionally Baptists have spoken of this dual commitment in terms of a 'covenant'. It is this covenant theology which lies behind the Baptist concept of church membership.

Contrary to popular opinion, Baptists do not believe in an individualistic approach to the Christian faith. The very reverse is the case: for where Baptists are true to themselves, then they have a very high doctrine of the church. Hence their stress on the responsibilities and privileges of church membership.

Many coming from other Christian traditions find the Baptist emphasis on church membership somewhat strange. In an Anglican or Roman Catholic church, membership is much less clearly defined. For instance, it is sometimes difficult to define a member of the Anglican church. Is it someone who has been baptised, or is confirmation also necessary? Is membership to be equated with registration on the parish electoral roll or attendance at Easter communion?

By contrast in a Baptist setting there is no room for doubt. Thus in a British context admittance to church membership usually involves a series of stages: after the initial application, the candidate is interviewed by representatives of the church; a report is brought to the church meeting and the candidate duly voted upon;

finally, the candidate is admitted to church membership with the 'right hand of fellowship', normally given at a celebration of the Lord's Supper. As we have already seen, church membership also normally presupposes believer's baptism.

> **TO THINK ABOUT . . .**
>
> **Is it true that Baptists have little difficulty identifying who are or who are not members of their churches?**
>
> **Is the author's case fair with respect to 'other Christian traditions', or can you argue differently?**

From the start, however, it is important to stress that for Baptists church membership goes far beyond admittance to a church roll, but is rather a dynamic process – it is, as the title of this chapter suggests, about 'living together in community'. Although Baptist churches may have their constitutions, these are not at the heart of the Baptist understanding of church membership. First and foremost church membership is about covenant relationships. It is this relational model of church membership which undergirds the radical nature of the Baptist way of being the church.

> **TO THINK ABOUT . . .**
>
> **What consequences ought to follow from membership of a Baptist church having more to do with living and covenant relationships than with just having your name on a church roll?**

What are the Scriptural grounds for this Baptist understanding of church membership? Is church membership, as understood by Baptists, a necessary expression of a person's commitment to Christ, or is it possible to belong to a church without being a church member? To help answer such questions we will consider some basic New Testament principles.

JESUS CALLS US INTO COMMUNITY

In the first place church membership is our response to the call of Jesus to belong to a community. For Jesus did not simply call people to follow him, he called them to follow him *together*. The actual term 'church' is only found twice in the Gospels (Matt 16:18; 18:17), but the thought is implicit throughout (see, for instance, the metaphors of 'flock' and 'vine' in John 10 and 15).

It is implicit not least in the fact that Jesus chose twelve disciples. Twelve was not just a fortuitous number, it was the number of the tribes of Israel. By choosing twelve men to follow him, Jesus was declaring to the world that he was in the process of recreating the people of God.

Neither is it a matter of chance that the first reference we have to the term 'church' comes in the context of Peter's confession of faith (Matt 16:16–18). It was in response to Peter's declaration that Jesus said: 'you are Peter, and on this rock I will build my church'. Personal faith and membership of the new community, the church, go hand in hand. Neither can be separated from the other.

Commitment to Christ, therefore, inevitably involves commitment to his people and church membership. In this sense Cyprian, one of the early church fathers, was right when he declared: 'Outside the church there is no salvation.' It is not that a person is saved by becoming a church member, but rather that church membership inevitably accompanies salvation. As Paul discovered on the Damascus Road, Christ cannot be separated from his people – for the question 'Saul, Saul, why do you persecute me?' (Acts 9:4) revealed that to persecute Christ's followers was tantamount to persecuting Christ himself. To put the same truth another way, when through faith in Jesus we are 'born again', we become members of the family of God. Personal faith has a corporate dimension.

TO THINK ABOUT . . .

What do Acts 2:41–42 and 1 Corinthians 12:13 say about a link between personal faith and membership of the Christian community?

This analogy of the church as a family also brings out the truth that our relationship with one another in the church is a gift from God and not a matter of personal choice. Just as in a human family we may find ourselves with brothers and sisters who belong to us, whether we like it or not, so too in the family of God we find ourselves surrounded by brothers and sisters in Christ, none of whom we have chosen, but nonetheless all of whom belong to us and we to them. In the world at large we may be able to pick and choose our friends, but in the church our brothers and sisters have been given to us by God. Such is the nature of Christian community.

TO THINK ABOUT . . .

How does the principle that in the church 'we may find ourselves with brothers and sisters who belong to us, whether we like it or not', apply in practice, for example to membership of a church housegroup?

*'As we prepare to share the Lord's Supper, my theme this morning
is the privilege of fellowship in the Body of Christ.'*

Furthermore, membership of this new community has definite and clear boundaries. This is evident in Jesus' other reference to the term 'church'. In the context of the brother who sins and refuses to heed brotherly admonition, members of the new community are called to 'tell it to the church; and if he refuses to listen even to the church, treat him as you would a pagan or a tax collector' (Matt 18:17). Church discipline implies church membership. It is not without significance that 'discipline', along with the 'preaching of the Word of God' and the 'administration of the sacraments', was seen by early Baptists, as well as by the Reformers in general, as an important, and for some an essential, feature of the church.

BAPTISM INITIATES US INTO COMMUNITY

For Paul, baptism was not merely a personal confession of faith, it was also a rite of initiation into the body of Christ, that is the church. Thus to the Corinthians he wrote: 'For we were all baptised by one Spirit into one body' (1 Cor 12:13). But Paul was not alone in seeing a corporate dimension to baptism. Luke concludes his account of the Day of Pentecost with the words: 'Those who accepted his [Peter's] message were baptised, and about three thousand were added to their number that day' (Acts 2:41). Baptism initiated these new converts into a community. This thinking is paralleled elsewhere – for instance, in Jewish proselyte baptism those Gentiles who were baptised were seen as identifying themselves with the people of Israel.

LOCAL CHURCH – UNIVERSAL CHURCH

For some, the point of issue, however, is the extent to which baptism initiates a person into the local church, as distinct from the church universal. How real a question would this have been for members of the early church? To them the local church was the expression of the church universal. It was unthinkable to belong to the one without belonging to the other. 'Now you are the body of Christ' (1 Cor 12:27) wrote Paul to the church at Corinth. Note the subject: 'you'. The apostle was not asserting that the church at Corinth was part of the wider church – it *was* the church – in Corinth. And so to be baptised into the body was to be baptised into the expression of the body of Christ in Corinth.

Church membership for the first Christians was no optional extra. It was inevitable. Free-wheeling Christians not meshed into the life of a local congregation simply did not exist. Just as it is impossible to belong to the army without belonging to a particular unit, so from a New Testament perspective it is inconceivable to belong to the wider church without belonging to a particular local unit.

WIDE CHOICE – NO CHOICE

For us, of course, the situation is bedevilled by choices not open to the first Christians. We can choose between this church and that, whereas the first Christians had only one church to which to belong. That does not invalidate the fact that church membership has little meaning unless it involves active participation in the life of a local church. The local church is the expression of the wider universal church. This point is brought

out well in the 1948 Baptist Union *Statement on the Church*:

It is in membership of a local church in one place that the fellowship of the one holy catholic Church becomes significant. Indeed, such gathered companies of believers are the local manifestation of the one Church of God on earth and in heaven. Thus the church at Ephesus is described, in words which strictly belong to the whole catholic Church, as 'the church of God, which He hath purchased with His own blood' (Acts 20:28). The vital relationship to Christ which is implied in full communicant membership in a local church carries with it membership in the Church which is both in time and eternity, both militant and triumphant. To worship and serve in such a local Christian community is, for Baptists, of the essence of Churchmanship.

TO THINK ABOUT . . .

Are churches which do not automatically link baptism with church membership being true to their roots or to Scripture?

How do you respond to the argument that an individualistic approach to baptism fails to understand the importance of community in Christian faith in general and Baptist life in particular?

Can you imagine any situation where it would be right to baptise someone without that person becoming a church member? If so, how do you argue for that practice?

THE LORD'S SUPPER PRESUPPOSES COMMUNITY

The Lord's Supper is a re-enactment of the Last Supper of Jesus with his disciples. On that occasion Jesus gave his disciples bread and then wine with the words, 'This is my blood of *the covenant*' (Mark 14:24). In the Jewish context of a Passover meal, a covenant implied a covenant people. Jesus, in establishing a new covenant, was recreating the people of the kingdom – the church that was to inherit the kingdom and be its instrument. The Lord's Supper was never intended to be a private rite. First and foremost it was – and is – a fellowship meal, and that presupposes community.

The communal aspect of the Lord's Supper is clearly expressed in 1 Corinthians 11:17–34, and in particular verses 27 and 29:

> whoever eats the bread or drinks the cup of the Lord in an unworthy manner will be guilty of sinning against the body and blood of the Lord . . . For anyone who eats and drinks without recognising the body of the Lord eats and drinks judgment upon himself.

Paul criticised those Corinthians who through their social divisions failed to express their oneness in Christ around his Table. 'The Lord's body' referred to here is the body of Christ, the church. They failed to realise that the whole church is the body of Christ.

Those who refuse to become church members, and yet who eat the Lord's bread and drink from his cup, make a similar mistake. They want to share in the family meal and yet refuse to be part of the family; they want the privileges of church membership, but not the responsibilities. This is not Christ's way.

This is not an argument for closing the Lord's Table to all but members of one local church – or, for that matter, closing the Table to all but those who have been baptised as believers. The Table surely must be open to 'all who are in good standing' with their own local churches, wherever and whatever they might be. The important point is that the Lord's Supper presupposes community. It is the fellowship meal of the committed.

Such commitment 'to one another' is expressed through church membership. In most Baptist churches this commitment is then symbolised through extending 'the right hand of fellowship'. This practice dates back to New Testament times. In Galatians 2:9 we read how James, Peter and John gave to Paul and Barnabas 'the right hand of fellowship'. In other words, they recognised them as fellow workers in the gospel. This is what 'the right hand of fellowship' is still about: a recognition of our oneness of spirit and purpose.

> **TO THINK ABOUT . . .**
>
> Does the phrase 'all who are in good standing' with their own local churches satisfy your criteria for who should attend the Lord's Supper?
>
> Do Baptists today need to think again about 'fencing' the Table?

THE CHURCH MEETING IS A CHARISMATIC EXPRESSION OF COMMUNITY

Church membership is viewed frequently in terms of attendance at church meetings, whether they are held monthly, bi-monthly or quarterly. Some see this as the essence of church membership. Just as the constitution of the Athenian 'ecclesia' or '(political) assembly' was democratic, with all citizens having equal right of speech and vote, so it is often argued that the constitution of a Baptist church is democratic, with all members having equal right of speech and vote.

But this is a false understanding of church membership and the church meeting. Because of the importance of the subject, we shall deal with the church meeting later in greater detail.

Suffice it to say here, the church meeting is not a democratic institution – but 'theocratic' in nature. In the words of the Baptist Union 1948 *Statement on the Church*, the church meeting:

> is the occasion when, as individuals and as a community, we [the members] submit ourselves to the guidance of the Holy Spirit and stand under the judgement of God that we may know what is the mind of Christ.

The members come together to seek *God*'s will, and not *their* will. The church meeting is not an occasion when rights may be exercised, but rather when gifts may be used. For God gives various gifts to his church – gifts, for instance, of leadership and discernment, of wisdom and prophecy. At a church meeting we share these gifts as we seek to discern the mind of Christ for our life together. It is no exaggeration to say that the church meeting is a charismatic expression of community.

TO THINK ABOUT . . .

Recall some specific issues on agendas of recent church meetings you have attended.

How were those issues handled?

How was each occasion used (or how could it have been used) to discover the mind of Christ rather than the will of individuals?

MEMBERSHIP IS COMMUNITY

RESPONSIBLE CHURCH MEMBERSHIP

There is a danger that sometimes church membership can be perceived as static – to be entered upon and then left behind. Thus in becoming a church member you become a name on a roll. But that is an inadequate view. Church membership is dynamic and carries ongoing responsibilities. For some Baptists, these ongoing responsibilities revolve around the church meeting. They view church membership primarily in terms of having a right and a duty to attend such meetings and to exercise their votes accordingly. But, as we have seen, this is a blinkered view.

First and foremost church membership is about commitment to Christ, which in turn leads to commitment to one another. This commitment to one another may be expressed through the church meeting. Thus John Smyth, in his pre-Baptist, Independent days, wrote of the church meeting:

> If you knew the comfort and power of the Lord's ordinances of admonition and excommunication as we do (blessed be our God) in some measure, and that growth and reformation which is in some of us thereby, you would be so wonderfully ravished with the power of God's ordinances, that you would acknowledge the Church to be terrible as an army with banners, and yet amiable and lovely, comely and beautiful.

Such an understanding of the church meeting is alas far removed from many Baptists today, for whom the church meeting centres upon *issues*, whether they be finance, fabric, or mission. For the first Baptists, church meetings centred on *people* – hence, as we have seen, their pre-occupation with matters such as church discipline.

SMALL GROUPS

In many Baptist churches today the 'home/fellowship group' has taken over some of the activities of the church meeting, as originally understood. This in itself may not be a backward move, provided it is understood that in such small groups we are exercising the 'responsibilities and privileges of church membership'. In any church larger than, say, fifty members, such fellowship groups are of the essence of its life together. Only as a church is broken down into small groups can people begin to relate together and meet one another's needs. Ideally every church member should relate to a fellowship group and through the group relate to others. Fellowship groups are vital, because only in such a context can meaningful fellowship be expressed: love can be displayed, life can be shared, maturity can be developed, gifts can be discovered. All this, reflected in the New Testament teaching of 'one anotherness' (see John 13:34–35; 1 Cor 12:25; Gal 6:2; Eph 4:15–16; 1 Thess 5:11; James 5:16), is church membership.

'Well, I thought they would at least allocate members to house groups according to which side of the main road we came from.'

COVENANT AND COMMUNITY

AN EARLY EMPHASIS

Our Baptist forefathers talked of covenanting together. Thus John Smyth and his followers at Gainsborough in 1606 covenanted together:

> to walk in all Christ's ways made known, or to be made known unto them, according to their best endeavours, whatsoever it should cost them.

Smyth defined a 'visible community of saints' as

> two or more joined together by covenant with God and themselves . . . for their mutual edification and for God's glory.

God covenanted to be their God, while Christians entering this covenant agreed to obey all God's commandments. Christians also had a duty to each other as believers, which Smyth termed 'the duties of love'.

This concept of church membership as entering upon a covenant together was very common in earlier days. In the Baptist church at Frome, Somerset, for example, prospective members had to subscribe to a three point covenant. These were (i) to be regular in worship; (ii) to care and be cared for in the Lord; and (iii) to accept financial responsibility for the ministry.

A CONTEMPORARY NEED

Baptist churches today often draw up a list of 'privileges and responsibilities of church membership' (see below), but frequently the notion of covenant is missing. Without the underlying concept of commitment to one another, which is of the essence of a church covenant, these lists of 'privileges and responsibilities' risk becoming rule-centred rather than people-centred.

The following are samples of statements of privileges and responsibilities currently used in Baptist churches.

(1) *Privileges and responsibilities of membership*

- Worshipping regularly with the people of God.
- Reading the Bible daily.
- Praying continually.
- Belonging to a small group.
- Discerning God's will for his people.
- Serving one another.
- Giving to God's work.
- Witnessing to God's love.
- Living a holy life.

(2) Responsibilities of a church member

- To live a life consistent with the Gospel and worthy of his or her high calling in Christ.
- To spend some time every day in prayer and reading the Scriptures.
- To share every Sunday, unless unavoidably prevented, in the corporate worship of the church.
- To accept personal responsibility for the government of the Church by attendance at the Church Meetings.
- To take some part in the work of the Church according to his gifts and opportunities.
- To live in fellowship with all the other members of the Church, serving one another in love.
- To set aside a realistic proportion of his income for the work of God carried on in and through the Church.
- To introduce others to the fellowship of the Church and engage in corporate and personal evangelism.

TO THINK ABOUT . . .

The church agreed wholeheartedly that its life and mission would be strengthened by drawing up a statement of the privileges and responsibilities of church members.

Ann, as the church's minister, felt it would be right and helpful to ask each member to go away from the church meeting and compile a list to be submitted to the deacons and herself for consideration.

Was Ann wise in the way she implemented the task?

What list of privileges and responsibilities would you have submitted if it had been your church?

As Baptists we need to rediscover our roots and realise afresh that, in becoming church members, we enter into a covenant together, a covenant which ultimately involves what some have called 'covenant relationship'. This is the logical consequence of our response to the new covenant that God has established with us through his Son's life, death and resurrection, and through sending the Holy Spirit: he has covenanted with us to be our God, we have covenanted to belong to one another in the Body of Christ. Just as David and Jonathan made a covenant together (1 Sam 18:3–4) and thereby strengthened one another's hands in God (1 Sam 23:15–16), so too we are called as church members to enter into such a relationship with others that we too can strengthen one another's hands in God. For this reason some churches call their small groups 'covenant groups'.

CHURCH DISCIPLINE

It is in fact only within the context of covenant relationships that meaningful church discipline can be exercised. In many Baptist churches today church discipline is exercised only when any hope of meaningful fellowship is gone and we remove the offender from our membership roll. But this is a caricature of church discipline. As earlier generations of Baptists well understood, church discipline is an aid to spiritual growth, and not a sign of spiritual death. Discipline is not a form of punishment, but rather is remedial in intent. Paul could write: 'if someone is caught in a sin, you who are spiritual should restore him gently' (Gal 6:1). Discipline – along with encouragement – is an expression of loving care. 'Truth', however, can only be spoken – and indeed, received, 'in love' within the context of covenant relationships. Furthermore, discipline needs to be exercised not just towards the 'grosser' sins of adultery or dishonesty, but also toward the less overt sins of pride and envy, which can sometimes be even more disruptive of Christian fellowship.

Ron Sider, who though not a Baptist links into our Anabaptist roots, throws light on a further aspect of covenant relationships when he defined true Christian fellowship as:

> an unconditional availability to and unlimited liability for the other brothers and sisters, emotionally, financially and spiritually (*Rich Christians in an Age of Hunger*, Hodder & Stoughton, London 1987, p164).

This is surely what church membership is all about. Certainly this is how Luke describes church membership in the opening chapters of the Acts of the Apostles. Thus those who accepted Peter's message on the day of Pentecost were baptised and added to the church (Acts 2:41) and then devoted themselves to the fellowship (Acts 2:42).

If this is true, it means that when we vote people into membership at our church meetings we are committing ourselves to them, to stand by them and love them, whatever the cost. This is a radical concept of church membership – but true to the New Testament Scriptures and true also to our roots. Baptists are radical believers!

TO THINK ABOUT . . .

Tony hadn't tried to hide it. He had admitted to the incident, and Roger, the pastor, knew it was a matter for church discipline and many hours of pastoral counselling.

He wasn't helped by the conflicting 'wisdom' of two experienced deacons. Martin told Roger that in every case of church discipline it was kinder and in the best interests of all if the leadership dealt with the matter. Joan told the pastor that she believed that in most cases, with few exceptions, the church meeting should be the place in which matters of church discipline were shared and resolved.

Who do you think had the stronger case? How should Roger proceed from here?

5

Living Under the Lordship of Christ

– authority among Baptists –

GOD RULES HIS PEOPLE

THEOCRACY

Democracy – 'government of the people, by the people, for the people' – in the world of politics is an ideal to treasure. But in the church this ideal does not apply. 'Jesus is Lord' we declare: his will and his will alone must reign supreme. If so, then any church laying claim to be a Christian church cannot operate on purely democratic principles. It will rather seek to pattern its life on 'theocratic' lines: i.e. it should seek to be ruled by God. 'Seek first [God's] kingdom and his righteousness' (Matt 6:33) – this will be the dominating motive as we live our lives together.

But what does it mean to be a theocracy? How does God rule his people. On this point Christians are divided. The following are the main views on the issue:

- God rules through bishops (**episcopacy**);
- God rules through elders (**presbyterianism** – found not only in Presbyterian churches, but also in 'house' or 'new' churches;
- God rules through church councils (**connexionalism**, as practised for instance in Methodism);
- God rules through church meetings made up of members of a local church (**congregationalism**).

CONGREGATIONALISM

It is this model which Baptists, along with Congregationalists, have usually adopted. John Smyth, for instance, argued that it is the congregation, 'saints as kings', who rule the visible church. Unfortunately congregational church government is often confused with democratic church government – in the same way that believers' baptism is often confused with adult baptism. However, as the Congregational theologian P.T. Forsyth once wrote, congregationalism 'was the mother of political democracy, but not its child'. To say that God rules through his people gathered together in church meeting is not to say that God rules through the ordinary democratic process. Rather, in the fine words of the 1948 *Statement on the Church*, the church meeting

> is the occasion when as individuals and as a community, we submit ourselves to the guidance of the Holy Spirit and stand under the judgements of God that we may know what is the mind of Christ.

Or, to adopt another definition, the church meeting is:

> the place where all members meet together regularly and, in an atmosphere of prayer, share their deepest spiritual concerns and seek the guidance of the Holy Spirit about all the matters which affect their common life as the family of God (Daniel Webster).

TO THINK ABOUT . . .

Democracy, as a political system, owes much to early Nonconformists, Baptists included.

Why is it helpful to favour this system of decision-making in the world of politics but unhelpful to see it as a model for decision-making in the church?

THE LOCAL CHURCH'S AUTHORITY

For Baptists the church meeting is paramount. This in turn has major implications as far as wider denominational life is concerned. If ultimate authority is in the members of a local church, meeting together in the name of Christ, then all forms of hierarchy are inevitably swept away. Whereas other churches are pyramidical in structure, with a pope, an archbishop, or a chairman of conference at the 'top', in a Baptist church the pyramid is inverted. The church is not subject to any human authority figure, whether within or without the church: rather the church is *served* by deacons, elders, pastors, and indeed by other church officials beyond the local church.

From this understanding of the local church the Baptist Union of Great Britain, in its declaration of principle, states as its first basis of union:

> That our Lord and Saviour Jesus Christ, God manifest in the flesh, is the sole and absolute authority in all matters pertaining to faith and practice, as revealed in the Holy Scriptures, and that each Church has liberty, under the guidance of the Holy Spirit, to interpret and administer His Laws.

A Baptist church is a self-governing church. Although, as we shall see in a further chapter, it will associate with other Baptist churches and thus express very real interdependence, it always possesses independency of judgement and decision. This Baptist practice of church government puts all the emphasis on the local church. Indeed, Baptists will not speak of their denomination as a *church*, but rather a *union* of churches. The local church is where the heart of Baptist life is found.

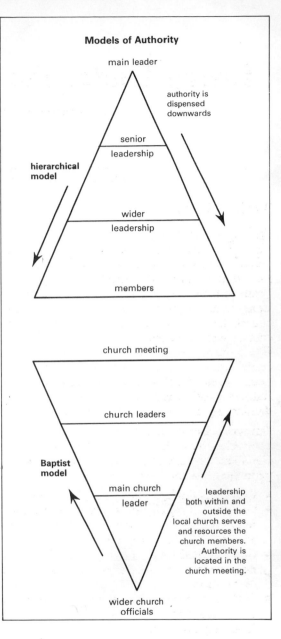

Models of Authority

main leader

authority is dispensed downwards

senior leadership

hierarchical model

wider leadership

members

church meeting

church leaders

Baptist model

main church leader

leadership both within and outside the local church serves and resources the church members. Authority is located in the church meeting.

wider church officials

THEOLOGICAL PRINCIPLES

No thinking Baptist would claim that the 'congregational model' is exactly patterned on the New Testament church. In the first place, nobody knows for sure how the early church operated – the minute books of the Jerusalem church, for instance, are unfortunately not open to inspection! In the second place, it is clear that church structures varied from place to place. What was possible in Jerusalem was hardly possible in Asia Minor – there were not twelve apostles for every church! On the other hand, there are certain principles enshrined in the New Testament which Baptists believe remain valid for today.

THE LORDSHIP OF CHRIST

First and foremost the church is not, as some Baptists have argued, 'the fellowship of believers'. It is rather, in the words of J.H. Oldham, 'Jesus Christ at work in the world through the fellowship of redeemed sinners'. Or put more simply in biblical terms, the church is the body of Christ (1 Cor 12:27; Eph 4:12), the bride of Christ (Rev 19:7), and the temple of the Holy Spirit (1 Cor 6:19). The church, whether local or universal, is only the church in so far as it relates to Christ as its Redeemer and its Head (see Eph 4:15; Col 1:18). The church cannot therefore be reduced to a purely human organisation. This means that in its life together the church is called to be neither democratic (ruled by the majority) nor despotic (ruled by the powerful few), but Christocentric (ruled by Christ). Jesus must be Lord!

> **TO THINK ABOUT . . .**
>
> **Is the author's criticism of the term 'fellowship of believers' valid?**
>
> **Does the term necessarily put too much emphasis on the church as 'a purely human organisation' and so divert attention away from understanding the church as the creation and agent of Christ?**

THE PRIESTHOOD OF ALL BELIEVERS

This principle, stated in 1 Peter 2:4–5, 9, declares that the age-old distinction between priest and people has been superseded. We are all priests – indeed in the letter to the Hebrews, all Christians are by implication high-priests (see, for instance, Heb 10:19–22).

In our relationship with God this means that there is no need for any human mediator: Jesus is the one mediator (1 Tim 2:5). In spiritual terms we are all equal before God. No one group has a greater claim on the Holy Spirit than another. In our relationship with others we are

Some thought the diaconate a smidgeon too authoritarian.

called to represent Christ to one another and the world. For this is the priestly task: to build bridges between God and his world.

In the light of these two aspects of priesthood, there is good reason for believing that every church member can be open to God and his Word. No one spiritual elite can claim to have a special hot-line to God.

THE MINISTRY OF ALL BELIEVERS

A number of passages could be cited supporting this doctrine, but the chapter which particularly comes to mind is 1 Corinthians 12. Here Paul develops the picture of the church as a body. God, says Paul, has so designed the body that the involvement of every person with his or her special gift is necessary for the proper functioning of the community. Every member has a unique role to play: the body is weaker where members withdraw and do not play their parts. Yes, there are particular leadership roles given by God to certain individuals, but these individuals do not have a monopoly of the Holy Spirit. For best results, all God's people are needed, pulling together.

THE CHURCH MEETING IN THE NEW TESTAMENT

The theological principles outlined above are reinforced by Luke's description of the early church in action. When decisions of fundamental importance had to be made, the whole church was involved in seeking the mind of Christ. Three passages come to mind, each concerned with a particular issue.

APPOINTING OFFICERS – ACTS 6

When the first 'deacons' were appointed, it was left to the church – and not to the apostles – to choose seven men

> known to be full of the Spirit and wisdom . . . They presented these men to the apostles, who prayed and laid their hands on them (Acts 6:3–6).

Surely it is not anachronistic to say that the church meeting was involved? Indeed, it would appear that the church had the primacy in all arrangements relating to the appointment of the Seven.

Thus, although scholars debate whether or not the 'ordination' of the Seven was by the apostles or by the church in general (the original Greek is a good deal vaguer than the present NIV translation and in fact suggests that Luke was referring to the church, rather than the apostles only, laying hands on the Seven), there is no doubt that the ceremony was very much under the direction of the church. The church meeting did not simply have a *say* in the appointment of the Seven: it *made* the appointment.

ADMINISTERING FINANCE – ACTS 11

Having heard Agabus' word from the Lord:

> The disciples, each according to his ability, decided to provide help for the brothers living in Judea. This they did, sending their gift to the elders in Jerusalem by Barnabas and Saul (Acts 11:29–30).

It is, of course, dangerous to read into the silences of Scripture: nonetheless, it seems significant that the disciples, and not the elders alone, were involved in the decision-making process. The particular role of the apostles it appears was to carry the gift to Jerusalem.

ADMITTING MEMBERS – ACTS 15

At the Jerusalem Council, called to discuss the whole question of admission of Gentile members to the church, although the apostles and the elders took the initiative in thrashing the matter through, the church as a whole was involved in making the decision to welcome Gentile believers into their midst. Luke records that 'the apostles and the elders, with the whole church, decided' (Acts 15:22). Indeed, later in that chapter he quotes the letter from the Jerusalem Council, which describes that decision in terms of it seeming 'good to the Holy Spirit and to us' (Acts 15:28). God guided his people through prayerful discussion together.

Interestingly, Luke tells us that when Judas and Silas arrived in Antioch with the letter detailing the decisions of the Jerusalem Council, 'they gathered the church together and delivered the letter' (Acts 15:30). The fact that the church rather than the church leaders were apparently the primary recipients is surely of significance.

In other words, in the Acts of the Apostles, whether in the appointing of church officers, the administration of finance, or the admission of members, the whole church was involved. Of course, the apostles and elders had key roles to play, yet at the end of the day it was not they who 'ran' the church, but rather the church as a whole was involved in major decisions involving its life.

THE TEACHING OF JESUS

The experience of the early church, however, is not sufficient. Our final authority must surely be the Lord Jesus himself: Matthew's Gospel contains the foundational text for the church meeting, namely **Matthew 18:15–20**. When an erring brother refuses to listen to you, and you have further tried to speak to him in the presence of one or two others, then, says Jesus, you are to 'tell it to the church'. The church in this context has authority to 'bind' (GNB: 'prohibit') and 'loose' (GNB: 'permit'): that is, the church has the final authority to pronounce what is or what is not sin (Matt 18:18).

Here Jesus makes clear that ultimate recourse in discipline is not to the elders or other church leaders, but to the church itself. By inference, what is true of church discipline is also true of other issues that affect the church: the church has final authority in every matter which affects its life.

To these verses Matthew adds another saying of Jesus: 'Where two or three come together in my name, there am I with them' (Matt 18:20).

Although the primary application in the first instance is no doubt to the disciples' prayer for the sinner of vv15–17, the principle of Jesus' presence amongst his people cannot be confined to that particular situation. Jesus is present wherever and whenever his people gather in his name. With specific reference to the church meeting we may argue that the church's ability to make authoritative decisions rests upon the presence of the risen Christ in its midst. It is as Christ's people consciously meet in his name and seek his will in prayer that authority is found.

1 Corinthians 5 provides a clear example of the kind of church discipline Jesus had in mind. For Paul tells the church as Corinth:

> When you are assembled [i.e. in what we would call the church meeting] . . . hand this man over to Satan, so that the sinful nature may be destroyed and his spirit saved on the day of the Lord Jesus (1 Cor 5:4–5).

Note, the discipline Paul has in mind is to be exercised not by the elders but by the church. The final authority lies within the church meeting.

TO THINK ABOUT . . .

Does the evidence above convince you of the biblical basis for congregational church government?

Another British Baptist interprets the New Testament evidence differently:

> the emphasis is that those in leadership have a God-given responsibility for governing the church and are personally accountable to God for this ministry as those entrusted with the care of the flock (1 Pet 5:2; Heb 13:7).

How do you feel when people come to different conclusions about the teaching of the Bible on particular issues – angry, confused, challenged to find out for yourself, or some other feeling?

Does it matter to you that you have a share in the decision-making task of your church, or would you rather hand over that responsibility to the leaders? Is your answer shaped by the Bible, your temperamental preferences or how much you trust and respect your church leaders?

AUTHORITY

POWER TO THE PASTOR?

In recent years the question of 'authority' has become a central issue in Baptist churches. After a period when many a Baptist pastor was often more or less regarded as the paid servant of the church, there to fulfil every whim of the congregation, the pendulum has swung. There has arisen an emphasis on a pastor's calling to lead the people of God. Influenced in particular by charismatics within some of the 'new churches' (the so called 'house churches' which emerged as part of the 'Restoration' movement), Scriptures are appealed to which appear to give real 'power' to pastors and other church leaders.

THE BIBLICAL BASIS

The Apostle Paul writes:

> The household of Stephanas . . . have devoted themselves to the service of the saints. I urge you, brothers, to submit to such as these and to everyone who joins in the work and labours at it (1 Cor 16:15–16).

> we ask you, brothers, to respect those who work hard among you, who are over you in the Lord and who admonish you (1 Thess 5:12).

> The elders who direct the affairs of the church well are worthy of double honour, especially those whose work is preaching and teaching (1 Tim 5:17).

Similarly the unknown author of Hebrews writes:

> Obey your leaders and submit to their authority. They keep watch over you as men who must give an account. Obey them so that their work will be a joy, not a burden, for that would be of no advantage to you (Heb 13:17).

To these Scriptures we could also perhaps add Galatians 1, where Paul tells the Galatians that he – and by inference leaders in general – is in the first place a servant of God, and not a servant of men: for his commission is 'not from men nor by man', but from 'Jesus Christ and God the Father' (Gal 1:1); hence he concludes that if 'still

'We have a strong diaconate.'

trying to please men, I would not be a servant of Christ' (Gal 1:10).

Similarly in Ephesians 4:11 it is the risen Christ who 'gives' pastor-teachers to his church, which in turn means that it is from Christ that pastor-teachers derive their authority. It is to Christ, therefore, that they owe allegiance.

SERVANT LEADERSHIP

These passages, however, are not as unambiguous as they might at first sight seem. Certainly, we cannot argue from them that the New Testament encourages any form of autocracy, where authority is imposed and unthinking obedience expected. Whatever authority Stephanas and his household enjoyed (**1 Cor 16:15–16**), it was clearly authority which derived not so much from their position as from the way they gave themselves in service to the church. What was true then is surely still true today: ultimately people obey their leaders not because of what they say but because of who they are. This is servant leadership.

Unfortunately some of our English translations of **1 Thessalonians 5:12** are more specific than is the original Greek text. Paul does not actually speak of the elders 'ruling', but rather of 'being over' God's people. Whereas the former term suggests power, the latter term is much softer in tone. Interestingly, the Greek verb here was used of a 'patron', one who had his clients' interests at heart – it was, for instance, used in connection with Phoebe's 'help to many people' in Cenchreae (Rom 16:1–2).

In **1 Timothy 5:17** the point at issue is not power but reward. The NIV and many other versions speak of double 'honour'; however, the GNB is almost certainly more accurate and speaks of 'double pay' for those who work hard at preaching and teaching. In many churches pastors would do well if they received salaries comparable with the average pay of their deacons, let alone twice the average!

Finally in **Hebrews 13:17**, although the writer undoubtedly expects the recipients of his letter to 'obey' their leaders, the Greek verb in question emphasises that blind obedience is not intended. The root meaning of the verb is 'to persuade', which in turn suggests that the author has in mind a response to reasoned exhortation rather than authoritarian command. Pastoral leadership in the New Testament is non-coercive; it leaves people free to accept or not accept its direction. Furthermore, Hebrews 13:17 should also be balanced by Hebrews 12:15, which clearly implies that the ministry of 'episcopal' oversight was shared by the whole congregation. A literal rendering of this verse, which as the context shows is addressed to the church as a whole (see Heb 12:14), gives the following translation: '[All of you] should exercise oversight (episkopountes) lest any one fails to obtain the grace of God.'

ACCOUNTABILITY OF LEADERS

Yet for all the above reservations, from a New Testament perspective leaders are clearly expected to lead. This leadership carries with it a certain authority which resides partly in the kind of people the leaders are but also in the role they are called to fulfil.

This, however, is not the full picture of authority within the local church. For although, as we have seen, leaders may be accountable to God (e.g. Gal 1:1, 10; Heb 13:17), they are also accountable to the church, which has recognised their calling and set them apart for service (Acts

'You-hoo! Budget time, Pastor. Are you there?'

13:1–3; 14:27). Hence, the church has the right not only to encourage its leaders, but also to admonish them. For example, Paul tells the church at Colossae to say to one of its leaders: 'See to it that you complete the work you have received in the Lord' (Col 4:17). Exhortation was not all one way! Honour and respect may be due to pastors and other church leaders, but there are times when they too need to be given direction – not by some outside 'apostle' but by the church which they serve.

In this respect the implications of Paul's account of his relationships with the apostles in Jerusalem is instructive (see Gal 2:1–2, 6–9, 11–14). The fact that Paul could rebuke Peter and Barnabas for hypocrisy in their dealings with Gentile Christians is a specific illustration of the more general truth that authority given to leaders must always be evaluated: are those leaders exercising their authority properly? If even Peter and Barnabas could get it wrong, then so too can Christian leaders today.

The fact is, as we have already seen, ultimate authority under God rests in the meeting together of the church's members, and not – as some would suggest – with the elders or other leaders within the church (Matt 18:15–20). Not surprisingly, therefore, we find in Luke's account of the early church that the church as a whole was involved in crucial questions relating to membership, leadership and finance (Acts 6, 11, 15). Similarly at Corinth we find the church taking the responsibility for disciplining a church member (1 Cor 5).

TO THINK ABOUT . . .

The church meeting had already spent over an hour discussing the possible appointment of a youth minister.

Rachel stood up and, expressing more than a little impatience said: 'Why can't we leave this matter to the deacons and elders to decide? After all, we set them apart to be our leaders. Shouldn't we give them freedom to lead us in what they believe is God's way for us?'

How would you respond to Rachel's comments?

LIVING WITH TENSION

In this matter of authority within the church there is very real tension: on the one hand, leaders are invested with authority; on the other hand, the church has ultimate authority. The question inevitably arises: how do we resolve this tension? The simple answer is that we cannot – or if we do, then immediately we become unbalanced and untrue to the teaching of the New Testament. We need to recognise that sometimes we have to live with tension in the Christian life.,

This is certainly true as far as some of the great doctrines of the faith are concerned. There is tension within the doctrine of the incarnation: Jesus is fully man, yet he is also fully God. Resolve the tension and immediately heresy is introduced. Tension is likewise present in the Christian doctrine of Scripture: it is inspired by God, yet it is written by people. Similar tension is found in the doctrine of 'free will' over against the doctrine of 'election'. Tension is inherent in our faith and cannot be avoided.

What is true of Christian doctrine in general is true likewise of our understanding of authority within the church.

Accountability does not rob the pastoral office of authority. Rightly understood, the church in appointing its leaders has delegated to them authority, authority which the leaders are free to exercise until the church withdraws its recognition of them. Leadership is a God-given role within the church: leaders are *serving the church* as well as their Lord in exercising their leadership gifts. A church, therefore, which refuses to allow its leaders to lead is rejecting God's gift to it of pastoral ministry (see Eph 4: 11–12), but this does not mean that church meetings simply rubber-stamp leaders' decisions. For leaders too are part of the Body of Christ, and their insights need to be tested along with those of others (1 Cor 12:10). They too are accountable to the church meeting.

On the other hand, a church will not lightly put to one side any recommendation coming from its leaders. On the contrary, any church meeting would need to think hard and long before overturning a unanimous recommendation of the deacons with regard, for instance, to its budget proposals for the forthcoming year.

However, no leaders are infallible – not even the pastor! The church meeting is the rightful place for testing all major proposals for church life, irrespective of from whom they come.

THE FINAL AUTHORITY IS CHRIST'S

Baptists in their life together have sought in various ways to give expression to the authority of the church meeting over against the authority of leaders. John Smyth, for instance, spoke of the church as:

the owner and primary possessor of the treasury, and the chief lord of it under Christ: and unto the Church must account finally be made.

Similarly he declared:

The body of the church, the spouse of Christ, ruleth as the wife under her husband, according to the will and appointment of her husband: the elders rule as the stewards of Christ the king, and of the church which is the wife or spouse of the king.

An example of this principle in practice is provided by the minutes of the Baptist church in Amersham, which in 1675 stated:

if Elder or Deacon or Elders or Deacons shall assume any power or prerogative above the Church and contrary to the words that the Church shall

judge and the Lord by his Word shall give the defined sentence; and if any difference fall out between Elder and Member or Deacon and Member and it be brought orderly to the Church they both shall stand by and the Church shall judge according to God's Word.

These examples illustrate that the early Baptist doctrine of the church meeting and their understanding of its authority was in no way confused with democracy. The church meeting was – and is – a means of discovering the mind of Christ. At the end of the day the final authority is Christ's. In the words of the declaration of principle of the Baptist Union of Great Britain, 'our Lord Jesus Christ . . . is the sole and absolute authority'; churches meet to 'interpret and administer *His* Laws'. 'Jesus is Lord' must ever be the motto of every church meeting.

TO THINK ABOUT . . .

'The church meeting is not a papal audience, nor is it a parliamentary battle ground. It is the family of God rejoicing in its response to visionary and loving leadership, in worship, in prayer, and in mutual submission to each other under God.'

Frank Cooke

How could your church meetings be reformed by this definition?

THE CHURCH MEETING IN ACTION

A DEMANDING AND EXCITING MODEL

The Baptist model of the church meeting is exciting. Every member has a part to play. Every member counts. Yet at the same time it is a highly demanding model. It expects much from the membership, and it expects much from the church meeting. At such meetings church business cannot be limited to rubber-stamping decisions relating to finance and fabric. Instead it involves seeking the mind of Christ in relation to all matters of faith and practice. In principle nothing is outside the orbit of the church meet-

ing, for nothing is outside the orbit of Christ. Matters of social and even political concern are all matters for a church meeting agenda.

This point needs emphasising. Church meetings worthy of their name are wide-ranging in character. The church's internal domestic concerns are not primary. Issues such as sex education and young people, the plight of the homeless, the mentally ill and community care, the challenge of AIDS to church and society, are on the agenda – along with other important issues such as developing an evangelistic strategy and the admission of new members.

'And so we come to tonight's major item of business: who should be allowed a key to the blue china cupboard.'

Consideration is given also to deploying effectively the gifts God has given his people. This involves not only discerning the gifts but also encouraging people to use them. Furthermore, a wise church will want to ensure that people exercise their gifts within the local community, and not just within the church. This in turn means that the church meeting will be involved not only in the selection and appointment of its leaders but also in the business of encouraging suitably gifted members to serve in the wider community, for instance, as magistrates, local councillors, or school governors.

In other words, church meetings need to focus on the larger issues of life. Matters of detail, such as the colour of the ladies' toilet and the state of the church kitchen, may be left to the deacons or some other appropriate sub-group within the church.

DISCOVERING THE LORD'S WILL

How in practice is the will of the Lord sought? At times the leadership will bring recommendations to the church. The church will normally accept these, unless there seem to be strong and compelling reasons not to. At other times members from the floor of the meeting will make suggestions or proposals. Clearly in the process of seeking the Lord's will some voices will carry more weight than others. People will listen with particular respect to those who are perceived to be 'mature' and 'spiritual'. And yet there are times when the Lord seems to by-pass even the 'wise' of the church. There must therefore be opportunity for all voices to be heard.

TO THINK ABOUT . . .

Ian had just been appointed a shop steward in the huge industrial plant near the church, and Avril had been appointed a magistrate.

Carol was determined that as their minister she would think of ways to help the members at the next church meeting to:

- understand the potential significance of these appointments;

- affirm Ian and Avril in their 'callings';

- devise ways of supporting and encouraging them in their 'ministry'.

How could the church members achieve these three goals?

At all times the views expressed by members must be carefully tested. It is not for nothing that, along with the gift of 'prophecy', the Lord gives 'the ability to distinguish between spirits' (1 Cor 12:10; see also 1 John 4:1). As part of that testing, the meeting may in its search for guidance cast votes. This need not be an unspiritual act. For unlike the normal democratic process, a mere majority in a meeting which is seeking the mind of Christ will never be sufficient. If Christ is guiding one, then he is likely to be guiding all. Consensus therefore is vital. In dealing with matters of any importance a considerable majority, perhaps 80% or more of those present, should believe that the particular course of action is of the Lord. If such a majority is not gained, then the proposition must be dropped and the will of the Lord further sought – if necessary at a subsequent church meeting.

> **TO THINK ABOUT . . .**
> Consider the merits or otherwise of another way of reaching consensus: occasionally introduce a second vote on an issue, when the minority has a chance to show acceptance of and support for a majority decision and so to own it themselves, even if earlier they had raised questions.
>
> The minority, dissenting group is then drawn into the consensus and is not left feeling 'outside'.
>
> What other ways could you commend for reaching consensus in a church meeting?

It is precisely because the actions and decisions of a church meeting transcend the normal democratic process that the custom of postal voting is inappropriate. This particular custom, found in some Baptist churches, arose from a desire to allow members unavoidably prevented from attending a church meeting (e.g. parents with young children, people away on business, the sick and the aged) to have their say on matters of particular importance in the life of the church. However, as has already been argued, the church meeting is not about having your say – it is rather about discerning the mind of

Christ. This process of discernment involves a sensitive listening to others and a careful weighing of what has been said. For Baptists decision-making of this kind is very much a corporate spiritual experience, in which the gathering together is an essential element in the prayerful discovery of the will of God (see Matt 18:20).

> **TO THINK ABOUT . . .**
> Does the author's argument about postal votes convince you? If not, what arguments persuade you that the voices of those absent from a church meeting should be counted in decision-making?

FREQUENCY AND TIME

Baptist churches vary as to the frequency of church meetings. Some hold them monthly, others only bi-monthly or even quarterly. The less frequently church meetings are held, the more they tend to degenerate into 'business' meetings preoccupied with the internal issues of the church, with little time for discussion of or reflection on some of the larger and more important issues. There is therefore much to be said for monthly church meetings. In this way agendas can be less full and a church can more genuinely engage in its task of discerning the mind of Christ concerning the varied aspects of its mission. Regular church meetings also aid better communication within the life of a church.

The frequency of church meetings is not the only matter to consider. The time at which they are held is also important. In Britain church meetings tend to be held during the week. However, with the increasing pressure of life, all mid-week meetings have been in decline – and correspondingly mid-week church meetings have also tended to be relatively poorly attended. Creative thinking is needed here. In other countries church meetings are often held on a Sunday – the provision of Sunday lunch, as also of activities for children, encourages a far higher turn-out.

'During the church meeting following the morning service and lunch, the children will be catechised by Brother Bernard.'

TO THINK ABOUT . . .

How often does your church membership gather for church meeting? Is it frequently enough?

Would your church respond positively to the idea of holding a church meeting on a Sunday? Why or why not?

What 'activities for children' would you favour?

THEMES FOR THE AGENDA

There is no one pattern for church meetings. By custom they begin and end with prayer. However, in so far as church meetings are an exercise in discerning the mind of Christ, there is much to be said for allowing prayer to permeate the whole meeting. Indeed, some churches stop half-way through their agenda and devote twenty or thirty minutes of prayer to matters already discussed or about to be dealt with.

Rather than setting out a standard church meeting agenda, it may be more helpful to list three items which are central to any church meeting agenda:

Worship

Time at the beginning of the meeting needs to be devoted to worship of the Lord whom the church seeks to serve and whose will she seeks to discern. Such worship will include not only hymns, songs and prayers, but also the reading of Scriptures relevant and appropriate to the agenda. God must be allowed to speak.

TO THINK ABOUT . . .

What are the strengths and weaknesses of holding church meetings as the church gathers around the Lord's Table?

Fellowship matters

Every church meeting should include opportunity for sharing news of the fellowship and for this news then to become fuel for prayer. Fellowship matters will also include applications for church membership – in British Baptist churches it is customary for two members of the church to visit the prospective member on behalf of the church and bring a brief report to the church meeting; in other countries it is sometimes the custom for prospective members to come to the church meeting to share their testimonies directly with the church.

Occasionally fellowship matters will include the sad business of church discipline: for just as it is the church which receives people into church membership, so it is the church which ultimately excludes people from membership. Clearly this latter action is only taken when the sin is gross and there is no evidence of repentance. (For further discussion of church discipline see page 56.)

Mission

A third item central to church meeting agendas is mission. Each agenda should contain at least one item relating to the mission of the church – whether it be evangelism or social action. The church must always be outward looking, remembering the world for whom Christ died.

Although everything else is secondary to the worship, fellowship and mission, there will always be other items on the agenda. There must always be opportunity for individual members to raise matters which are on their hearts. The church meeting is the ideal occasion for any 'words' from the Lord to be shared – and tested.

TO THINK ABOUT . . .

Do you agree with the author that items relating to mission should be on the agenda of every church meeting? How would you ensure discussion on the issues resulted in action and not just fine words?

THE CALLING OF A PASTOR

An illustration of the Baptist approach to authority is found in the way in which Baptist churches call their pastors. For unlike most other mainline churches, where a pastor's appointment is influenced from outside by ecclesiastical figures (e.g. bishops) or church councils (e.g. synods), albeit sometimes in consultation with representatives of the local church, amongst Baptists it is the local church itself which has the primary responsibility in calling its new pastor. True, in a British situation, churches will usually consult their area superintendent, who in turn will suggest a number of 'names' to the church. But it is entirely up to the church whether or not it feels right to follow up those suggestions.

How does all this work out in practice?

THE ROLE OF DEACONS

In Britain it is generally the deacons who initially act on behalf of the church, receiving names not only from the superintendent but also from church members and other sources. (Elsewhere this task is sometimes delegated to a specially constituted 'pastoral vacancy committee' or 'search committee'). However, before an approach is made to anyone, it is now customary to draw up a church profile. This in turn is submitted to the church meeting for its approval: this profile, amongst other things, normally speaks of the hopes and aspirations of the church for the next phase of ministry.

After the church has considered the profile, and the information gleaned about the various names given as potential future pastors of the church (sometimes through personal profiles submitted through the superintendent), individuals are then approached – always one at a time – with invitations to meet with the deacons to explore possibilities of future ministry. If such a meeting goes well and there seems to be a good 'match', the individual concerned is then invited to 'preach with a view' and meet with the church as a whole.

THE ROLE OF THE CHURCH

At this stage the matter is more or less out of the hands of the deacons. The deacons may meet to make a recommendation to the church meeting, but the actual decision in calling the person concerned rests now with the church, not with its leadership.

With the issuing of a 'call' the matter is not

finally resolved – the person being called is also involved in decision-making, with the result that the call only becomes a reality once both the church and the pastor-to-be are convinced that God is indeed in this call.

All this may sound complicated and time-consuming, and so it often is. No doubt the process of calling a pastor would be much simpler and swifter if the matter were left to some figure with 'apostolic' authority. But for Baptists such a procedure would run contrary to their perception of the way major decisions should be reached. Christ rules his church through his people, which in turn involves the church meeting.

TO THINK ABOUT . . .

Hazel was having coffee with Brian and Vicky on the evening after Simon had 'preached with a view'.

'I couldn't be at church yesterday as I was on duty all day,' said Hazel.

'He preached two terrific sermons,' said Simon.

'That may be,' said Vicky, 'but how do we know he understands our vision for the church's future?'

'I suppose,' replied Hazel, 'we have to trust the recommendation of the deacons, but it doesn't seem a very good system to me.'

Do you have some sympathy both with Hazel's circumstances on the Sunday and with her point of view?

How would you improve our system of calling ministers?

In early Baptist life pastors often had to spend time 'on trial' in a church, before being formally called to the pastorate. Is that a possible option today or are circumstances so different as to make it impractical?

'Next, marks for conduct of worship . . . Press your buttons now!'

IN CONCLUSION

Here again we have an example of Baptist radicalism. Baptists dare to entrust all the major decisions of their life together to the church as it meets in church meeting, believing that this is God's way for his people to discern the mind of Christ. Needless to say, there is no guarantee that the church meeting will always rightly discern Christ's mind. Church meetings can sometimes be dominated by the personal feelings of members rather than by a desire to do the Lord's will, whatever that involves. Indeed, there is no such thing as an ideal church meeting, for even the best we can offer God is spoilt by sin. Baptists do not always live up to their ideals, but that does not mean that an alternative and less radical model of decision-making should be adopted. Rather, as is true of the Christian life in general, Baptists are called constantly to become what by God's grace they already are – people living under the lordship of Christ.

The great Congregational preacher of times past, R. W. Dale, said: 'To be at church meeting is for me one of the chief means of grace'. Although Baptists cannot pretend this is true of all church meetings, they do believe that there is no finer instrument for discovering the mind of Christ. For those belonging to a local Baptist church, there are few greater privileges than helping to discover and decide what God would have his church be and do.

TO THINK ABOUT . . .

Does it matter who takes the chair at a church meeting?

In British Baptist churches the pastor normally chairs the meeting – in other countries it is often a deacon.

TO THINK ABOUT . . .

Can you imagine occasions when it would be helpful for matters normally restricted to the church meeting to be aired in an open forum (e.g. Sunday worship) where the whole congregation could be sounded out on an issue?

On what matters do you think your church might or ought to seek the mind, advice and support of other Baptists in your district or association?

6
Associating with Others

– Baptists are not independents –

THE BIBLICAL BASIS

Fellowship is the lifestyle of the gospel. By faith we are born again into the great family of God, a family which transcends all boundaries of race, culture and language. In the words of the Apostle Paul, in the fellowship of the church 'there is no Greek or Jew, circumcised or uncircumcised, barbarian, Scythian, slave or free' (Col 3:11) – for we are 'all one in Christ Jesus' (Gal 3:28). Not surprisingly, Luke describes 'fellowship' as one of the hallmarks of the life of the early church (Acts 2:42).

This fellowship in the gospel cannot be restricted to Christians worshipping together in one locality. No individual Christian can afford to be a loner, neither can any local church afford to go it alone. If a local church goes its own way regardless of other churches, then by its very individualism it is denying the fullness of the gospel. A church which fails to live in fellowship with others is a gross mismutation, and is no longer a living cell within the wider body of Christ.

TO THINK ABOUT . . .

Before getting into this chapter, note down in what ways your church has links with other congregations in your local community, in your Baptist association, or wider afield.

What do you learn about your church from that exercise?

An examination of the New Testament quickly reveals that the young churches had a very keen sense of belonging to a wider fellowship. Two examples come to mind in particular: one financial, the other doctrinal.

FINANCE

When the mother church in Jerusalem suffered economic hardship, the daughter church rallied round and took up a noteworthy collection (1 Cor 16:1–4; 2 Cor 8:1–9, 15; Rom 15: 25–28). Indeed, the underlying Greek word 'koinonia' (fellowship) could be used in a concrete sense to denote a 'gift' or 'contribution': the 'collection' (koinonia) which Paul took up was a sign of fellowship (see Rom 15:26–27). Fellowship, if it has any meaning at all, has to be expressed, and that expression has no geographical limitations. Paul's injunction to the Galatians to 'do good to all people, especially to those who belong to the family of believers' (Gal 6:10) could not be restricted to any particular locality.

DOCTRINE

When a major issue of faith and practice cropped up in the church in Antioch, they decided to involve the mother church in Jerusalem and not deal with the matter by themselves. At the resulting 'Council of Jerusalem' the agreed guidelines were sent out not just to the church in Antioch but also to the churches in Syria and Cilicia (Acts 15:23). Clearly the churches had a corporate sense of identity. Fellowship in the gospel involved consulting with one another and coming to agreements with one another. Interdependency rather than independency was a hallmark of the early church's life.

LOCAL AND UNIVERSAL

Unfortunately some Baptists, in their desire to emphasise the importance of the local church, have sometimes fallen into the error of isolationism. It is true that the majority of references to the church in the New Testament have the local church in mind (according to one calculation, more than 100 of the 114 instances of the term 'ekklesia' (church) denote the local church), but this does not justify ecclesiastical isolationism. The church is at one and the same time both local and universal.

Hence for Paul, not only the local church (2 Cor 11:1–3) but also the universal church (Eph 5:25–33) is the bride of Christ. Likewise the local church (1 Cor 12:27) or the universal church (Eph 4:15, 16; Col 2:19) can be termed the body of Christ. Similarly, the writer to the Hebrews sees the local church in its worship opened up to the universal church (Heb 12:18–24). Baptists, with their radical perceptions of the local church, must also be mindful of the wider church.

BAPTISTS AND ASSOCIATING

ASSOCIATING LOCALLY

From almost the beginning Baptists recognised the importance of local churches 'associating' with one another. In 1644, for instance, representatives of seven Particular Baptist churches met together in London to produce a *Confession of Faith*. In the preamble to that Confession they underlined their conviction that

> though we be distinct in respect of our particular bodies, for conveniency sake, being as many as can well meet together in one place, yet all are one in communion, holding Jesus Christ to be our head and lord; under whose government we desire alone to walk.

Furthermore, this 'communion' was to receive concrete expression:

> And although the particular congregations be distinct and several bodies, every one a compact and knit city in itself; yet are they all to walk by one and the same rule, and by all means convenient to have the counsel and help one of another in all needful affairs of the church, as members of one body in the common faith under Christ their only head. (chapter XLVII)

At a meeting of church representatives at Tetsworth, Oxfordshire, in 1653, the churches signed an agreement acknowledging mutual interdependence and agreed to confer on three matters:

- advice on controversial matters which could not be resolved by one church on its own;
- the provision of financial support for any congregation in need;
- the common planning, for the greater glory of God, of anything which required 'the joint carrying on of the work of the Lord that is common to the churches'.

These three areas of co-operation parallel the early church: the first area is reminiscent of the Council of Jerusalem; the second recalls the collection for the Jerusalem poor; and the third may perhaps be compared to the decisions which emerged from the leaders' conference in Jerusalem when Paul, Barnabas and Silas met with James, Peter, and John, to discuss missionary strategy (Gal 2:1–10).

As far as the early Baptists were concerned, the principle of association beyond the local church was an extension of the privileges and responsibilities of fellowship within the local church. The church representatives meeting at Wormsley in October 1652, prior to the meeting at Tetsworth declared:

> There is a like relation betwixt the particular churches each towards other, as there is betwixt particular members of one church. For the churches of Christ do make up but one body or church in general under Christ their head . . . We conclude that every church ought to manifest its care over other churches as fellow members of the same body of Christ in general.

In other words, 1 Corinthians 12:12–27 has an application beyond the local church. The Body of Christ, of which we are part, is the wider church. Associating with other churches, therefore, is no optional extra – it is part of being the church.

TO THINK ABOUT . . .

'. . . by all means convenient to have the counsel and help one of another in all needful affairs of the church, as members of one body . . .'.

Why is it often difficult to get local churches to implement that ideal of early Baptists?

ASSOCIATING NATIONALLY

This emphasis on associating with one another became a Baptist distinctive. Historically and theologically Baptists have been committed to interdependency. The independence of the local church is not the be-all and end-all of Baptist life. True, 'each church has liberty, under the guidance of the Holy Spirit, to interpret and administer [God's] laws', but this extract from the Baptist Union of Great Britain's declaration of principle needs reading in context. That declaration is immediately followed by 'the objects of the Union', which under the general umbrella of 'the advancement of the Christian religion' are:

1) To cultivate among its own members respect and love for one another, and for all who love the Lord Jesus Christ.
2) To spread the Gospel of Christ by ministers and evangelists, by establishing Churches, forming Sunday-schools, distributing the Scriptures, issuing religious publications, and by such other methods as the Council shall determine.
3) To afford opportunities for conference, and for united action on questions affecting the welfare of the Churches, the support of the ministry, and the extension of the Denomination, both at home and abroad.
4) To promote fraternal relations between Baptists in this and other countries.
5) To obtain and disseminate accurate information respecting the organisations, labours and sufferings of Baptists throughout the world.
6) To confer and co-operate with other Christian communities as occasion may require.

In other words, churches in membership with the Baptist Union are not just committed to the principles enshrined within the declaration of principle, but also to the objects of the Union. Membership involves more than a commitment to a particular way of believing, it also involves commitment to the wider Baptist family and to other Christian communities.

ASSOCIATING TODAY

The local church apart, associating today may take place at a number of levels. For instance, apart from the Strict Baptists (who have formed their own associations) and various 'independent' Baptist churches in England and Wales, every Baptist church belongs to one of thirty-nine Baptist associations, and most Baptist churches also belong to the Baptist Union of Great Britain.

THE BAPTIST UNION

The Baptist Union of Great Britain is based at Didcot, Oxfordshire, and shares its premises with the Baptist Missionary Society. The Union has a staff spread over three interrelated departments of mission, ministry, and administration, and acts as a resource to its member churches and associations.

It needs to be emphasised that in the first place the Baptist Union is a mission agency. The Union is keenly aware that it exists not for the sake of itself, nor even primarily for the sake of its member churches and associations, but above all for the sake of the world for whom Christ died. The Baptist Union came into existence as a result of concern for mission, and mission remains its *raison d'etre*. Because of this emphasis the Baptist 'family purse' is rightly called the 'Home Mission Fund'. Not surprisingly, therefore, mission and evangelism come to the fore in the Baptist Union Council's statement of intent, adopted in March 1992.

Towards 2000 – The Statement of Intent

Seeking God's guidance through the holy Spirit, under the Lordship of Christ, and in response to the concerns of the churches, we, the Baptist Union Council, commit ourselves:

- to encourage, support and initiate imaginative and effective strategies in evangelism and other aspects of God's mission;
- to develop our distinctive Baptist identity;
- to strengthen our associating by mutual commitment at every level;
- to promote the greater sharing of people, money and other resources.

The relationship between the Union and the churches has been likened to that between the apostles and the churches expressed by Paul in 2 Corinthians 1:24:

> Not that we lord it over your faith, but we work with you for your joy, because it is by faith you stand firm.

Accountable in the first place to the Baptist Union Council, a sizeable body of about 210 people, representative of churches, colleges and associations, the Union is ultimately accountable to the annual Baptist Assembly.

Such accountability reflects the principle of the gathered community, which lies at the heart of

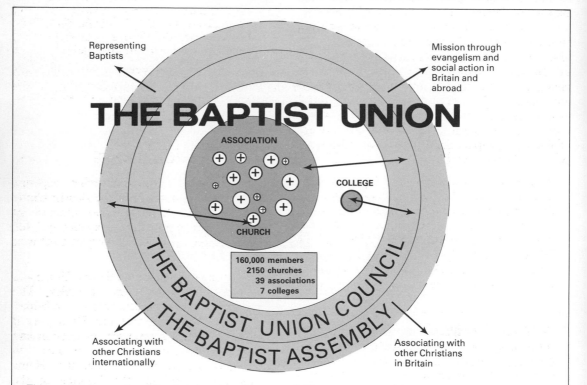

This model places a local Baptist church at the centre. It illustrates some of the structures and networks for associating within and beyond the Baptist Union of Great Britain.

A church associates most immediately with other churches in its local association. There are thirty-nine such associations, each represented on the Baptist Union Council, where all seven Baptist theological colleges are also represented through their principals.

Each of the 2150 churches in membership with the Baptist Union may send delegates to the annual Baptist Assembly.

The outer circle is a broken line to emphasise that the Baptist Union is not a closed, inward looking community. In varied ways it reaches out to others in mission, and associates with others beyond its membership.

Baptist church life. For as at local church level any decision of major importance is not made by the deacons or elders, but rather by the church meeting, so at national level any decision of major importance is made not by the Council but by the Assembly, which in Baptist thinking is the wider people of God gathered together to discern the mind of Christ on the issues of the day. As we shall see later in this chapter, it was, for instance, the Assembly – and not the Council – which committed the Baptist Union of Great Britain to become a member of the Council of Churches for Britain and Ireland.

Although a few voices in the Baptist Union call for the Council to have much greater power, a synodical form of government is foreign to the Baptist understanding of the church: Baptists are congregationalists – at every level of their life together. Indeed, in the light of this ecclesiology, you could argue that the present structure of Baptist Assembly meetings should be changed, so that they become less inspirational and more deliberative. This change would ensure that the Assembly returned to its radical roots and reflected more accurately the concept of assembly propounded by George Gould in the Norwich Assembly of 1879:

> We meet as a deliberative body of Christians, who, agreeing in the belief of evangelical truth, and desiring to maintain the ordinances of the Gospel as our Lord hath delivered them to us, take counsel together that we may act, as far as possible, in concert for the furtherance of the Gospel of Christ, and in promotion of the efficiency of our body through its various organisations.

> *TO THINK ABOUT . . .*
> **What position do you take on whether the Baptist Assembly should be largely inspirational or deliberative?**

Representing the Union in the field are twelve General Superintendents. Although we shall focus on their particular ministry later on, we should note that they have in their care twelve 'Areas'. Three of these areas are co-terminous with an association (the East Midlands, Lancs & Cheshire and London) – the other nine

include two or more associations. The heart of Baptist life, however, does not centre on areas, which are but administrative devices of the Union's making. By and large churches relate to their local association, not to their area.

> *TO THINK ABOUT . . .*
> **Pat, the church's pastor, was visiting Vi and Des the week after the Baptist Union President had preached.**
>
> **'He was good,' said Des. 'I admit I haven't really thought much about our belonging to the BU before.'**
>
> **'Yes,' chimed in Vi, 'it all seems a bit remote. And anyway, Pat, you've always told us that for Baptists the local church is what's important. How does that fit with this big central, bureaucratic machine called the Baptist Union? What's the point of it?'**
>
> **How might Pat helpfully reply?**

LOCAL ASSOCIATIONS

At a more local level Baptist churches cooperate together in associations. Like the Baptist Union itself, the associations are mission agencies. All the many other functions of associational life are, in principle at least, subservient to that of mission.

The relationship between the Baptist Union and the associations is somewhat complex. The association in many respects acts as the broker between the churches and the Union, as it mediates the Union's resources of mission and ministry to the churches. For instance, no church may receive money from the 'Home Mission Fund' without the backing of the association; no ministerial student can apply to a Baptist college without the commendation of the association. The association conducts 'mission audits' of local churches and thereby mediates the Union's 'Action in Mission' programme to the churches. The Union produces resources for study and training, for example through the Christian Training Programme, which the associations are encouraged to use and commend to the churches.

Some of the Union's resources of mission and ministry are also directly available to the local church. For instance, the movement of pastors is a Union rather than an association responsibility.

The local association is better placed to be more user-friendly than the Union, by virtue of being a regional rather than a national body. Whereas the latter only meets once a year in 'Assembly', when representatives of all the local churches are invited to meet together, the meetings of the former tend to be more frequent and more geographically accessible. The Baptist Assembly does move around the country from year to year, but inevitably this means that for most churches a visit by the Assembly is an occasional event.

Furthermore, the very size of the Assembly makes it for many a fairly daunting occasion – in smaller association assemblies it is easier to get to know people by name.

> **TO THINK ABOUT . . .**
>
> **Is the last sentence borne out in your experience or the experience of any you know who have attended Baptist assemblies or association meetings?**
>
> **May a weekend residential assembly offer better scope for getting to know people than, for example, an overpacked association evening?**

A RENEWAL OF ASSOCIATION LIFE

In principle the local association offers enormous scope for churches to work together for the extension of Christ's Kingdom. Sadly, in reality, many associations are creaking at the seams and in their structures have failed to adjust to the realities of the present. Although many churches have experienced renewal of one kind or another, associations have tended to be slower to respond to the pace of change. In the minds of most people associations are perceived as boring and irrelevant. Not surprisingly, many churches and individuals have voted with their feet, with the result that association officials bemoan the poor attendances at their meetings.

What can be done? Should 'the dead' be left to bury the dead? There are those who believe that the present situation is hopeless and who therefore seek fellowship and inspiration from alternative structures. However, if Baptist theology and history are at all meaningful, then the answer lies in our understanding of association. Associating with other churches is not an optional extra. As a result of the 'covenant' we have entered into in joining the association in the first place, churches are committed to one another. This does not mean we are committed to the present way of doing things. It does mean, however, that we are committed to finding a way of making associations meaningful in terms of ministry and mission.

> **TO THINK ABOUT . . .**
>
> **What truth is there in the argument that associations lose their way once mission and strategic planning for advance are moved from the centre of their agendas?**
>
> **If you agree, can you cite examples of the argument, and evidence of good association life in this respect?**

LEADERSHIP IS CRUCIAL

Although there is no one answer to the malaise which appears to affect some associations, the key to the renewal of association life is surely in its leadership. It is perhaps unfortunate that in many associations the full-time official is known as the association secretary, a term which inevitably conjures up the imagery of sober management, rather than of dynamic leadership. True, most associations have a 'president' or 'moderator', but this leadership position tends to be rotated on an annual basis, with the result that the office-holder is unable to achieve very much in his or her brief tenure of office.

To complicate matters, the area super-intendent is perceived as primarily an official of the Baptist Union (he is paid by them!) rather

'And we will send two divisions of the Wessex Association storm troopers to claim the ground around Lower Snodgrass-in-the-Marsh.'

than of the association (even although in his election the association had the majority of votes).

Many argue that superintendents should give a lead and act as generals to their troops, rather than as sick nurses to their charges. Leadership must become the priority. Of course, there will always be problem churches to trouble shoot, wounded pastors to counsel, and Baptists to represent on this committee and that. But just as wise pastors learn to delegate some of their tasks, so too must superintendents learn to delegate and concentrate on exercising visionary leadership.

Each superintendent needs around him a small strategy team, which in turn will play the equivalent role of a leadership team within the local church. And just as leadership within the local church functions best in the context of trust and encouragement, so too will leadership within the local association.

TO THINK ABOUT . . .

At the Wessexshire Association council meeting frustration began to boil over into some hard-hitting exchanges.

Dave, one of the association's younger ministers, as graciously as he could (without being very successful), turned on the meeting and declared: 'The leadership of the association is the key. Our association will be as visionary, forward-looking and dynamic as those who lead it.'

Basil, the association secretary, tried not to feel pained and irritated (though he was). He got to his feet and replied: 'The truth is, the association is strong or weak depending on the commitment of each member church and its leadership. Count how many churches are *not* represented here this evening and at most association occasions.'

Who has more truth on his side?

A RENEWED ASSOCIATION

On the agenda of a renewed association such items as church planting and cross-cultural mission would feature. Larger churches would be encouraged to send out faith-sharing teams to smaller churches – and vice versa. The pastoral care of pastors and other full-time Christian workers within the association would include annual appraisal interviews, when their work would not only be assessed but also fresh goals for personal development and growth would be set. Ideally the annual appraisal of pastors would also be conducted alongside the annual mission-auditing of local churches by outside 'consultants' appointed by the association. Short-term, task-orientated work groups would replace the apparently eternal committees.

Alongside celebrations and 'family-days' for all the churches, there would be such activities as weekends away for young people, music-making for instrumentalists, training for worship leaders, sharing of experiences for magistrates and school parent-governors. Unlike a local church, an association has tremendous resources of expertise – this expertise should be utilised for the building up of the church and for the extension of the kingdom. Everything is possible where imagination and creativity is harnessed with faith and with commitment. The dry bones of an association can live to become a mighty army!

> **TO THINK ABOUT . . .**
> Describe the structures or networks, linking together Baptist churches in your area, which you believe would best serve the ideals of associating and interdependence set out in the Scriptures and the early Baptist *Confessions*?

'They said they wanted some dynamic leadership, so he's rehearsing his power sermon for the association assembly.'

NETWORKS FOR ASSOCIATING

BAPTIST COLLEGES

The way Baptist churches in the United Kingdom have come together to provide theological education is a further example of associating. Today there are seven Baptist colleges in Bangor, Bristol, Cardiff ('South Wales'), Glasgow ('Scottish'), London ('Spurgeon's'), Manchester ('Northern'), and Oxford ('Regents Park'). All seven colleges are in membership with the Baptist Union of Great Britain, yet are at the same time independent bodies.

BAPTIST MISSIONARY SOCIETY

We shall focus later on the work of the Baptist Missionary Society. Suffice it to say, the BMS is a classic example of Baptists associating together for the purpose of mission. Founded in 1792, the BMS preceeded the founding of the Baptist Union – indeed, historians tell us that it was the formation of the BMS which provided the impetus for the formation of the first Baptist Union amongst Particular Baptist churches in 1812–1813.

The BMS today serves as the missionary society for the Baptist Union of Great Britain, the Baptist Union of Scotland, and the Baptist Union of Wales. It thus offers an opportunity for churches within three Baptist unions not only to associate with one another but also with the Baptist conventions and unions with which the BMS is in partnership overseas. (For further material on the Baptist Missionary Society, see page 109.)

BAPTIST WORLD ALLIANCE

Baptist forms of association go beyond regional and national boundaries. Currently there are 151 Baptist unions and conventions in membership with the Baptist World Alliance (BWA). Founded in London in 1905, the BWA is serviced by a small international resource staff based in Virginia, USA. The stated purpose of the Alliance is 'to impart inspiration to the fellowship [of Baptists], and to provide channels for sharing concerns and skills in witness and ministry'. The BWA has often played a major role in helping minority Baptist groupings gain recognition from governments hostile to the Christian faith. It is also active in providing help to third-world countries through its Baptist World Aid programme.

There are six regional fellowships for Baptists: the All-Africa Baptist Fellowship, the Asian Baptist Federation (this also includes Australia and New Zealand), the Caribbean Baptist Fellowship, the European Baptist Fellowship, the North American Baptist Fellowship, and the Union of Baptists in Latin America.

THE EUROPEAN BAPTIST FEDERATION

The European Baptist Federation (EBF) has a proud record of achievement, not least in helping its member unions in Eastern Europe. One of the EBF's current major responsibilities is the funding and oversight of the International Baptist Theological Seminary based in Rüschlikon, a Swiss village close to Zurich, as also its sister institution, IBLA (the International Baptist Lay Academy) based in Budapest, Hungary. Every five years European Baptists come together for a major congress, which is always rich in fellowship and inspiration.

TO THINK ABOUT . . .

As the countries of Europe forge even closer links, how could your church become more aware of Baptist life in Europe and develop stronger links with Baptist churches on the European mainland?

What may be some effective strategies for mission in Europe which Baptists could implement over the next few years?

ASSOCIATING WITH OTHER CHRISTIANS

So far we have focused on Baptists associating with one another – whether at association, national, or even international level. However, the same principles that motivate Baptists to associate together also motivate Christians in general to associate together.

THE ECUMENICAL MOVEMENT: A GOSPEL DEMAND

The modern ecumenical movement is normally dated from the Edinburgh Missionary Conference of 1910. This was the first really international conference of a multidenominational character, and although its theme was 'mission', inevitably the degree to which the various bodies represented could co-operate was never far off the agenda.

The seeds of ecumenism were found in mission. Rightly understood, unity has never been for the sake of unity but rather for the sake of mission. In this context the words of Jesus in the so-called 'high-priestly prayer' are important: 'I pray . . . that all of them may be one . . . so that the world may believe you have sent me' (John 17:20–26).

Mission is hindered by disunity. The Indian Christian leaders who came together at Tranquebar in 1919 – shortly after the Edinburgh Missionary Conference – declared:

> We face together the titanic task of the winning of India for Christ – one fifth of the human race. Yet confronted by such an overwhelming responsibility, we find ourselves rendered weak and relatively impotent by our unhappy divisions – divisions which we did not create and which we do not desire to perpetuate.

What was true in India then is surely still true the world over. It is difficult for Christians to preach a gospel of reconciliation and yet at the same time be unreconciled with one another.

TO THINK ABOUT . . .

'The existence of some nine thousand Christian denominations across the world is an insult to Christ, a denial of the gospel and the greatest hindrance to the spread of the Kingdom of God.'

(David Watson)

What is your response to that statistic and do you agree with David Watson's conclusion?

'My message this morning is on the theme of John 17:20–22 and the ecumenical movement.'

BAPTISTS AND ECUMENISM

Worldwide the Baptist response to the ecumenical movement has been cautious. Only a minority of Baptist unions and conventions are in membership with the World Council of Churches (WCC). Yet even those unions and conventions which feel unable to become formal members of the WCC recognise the need to relate to other denominations. Baptists cannot pretend that they alone are the Lord's people!

The Baptist Union of Great Britain has always had a positive attitude toward the ecumenical movement. One of the original founder members of the WCC in 1948, as also of the former British Council of Churches in 1942 (superceded in 1990 by the Council of Churches for Britain and Ireland – CCBI), the Baptist Union has always felt that the things that unite us are more important than the things that divide us, and that it could more effectively witness to its Baptist distinctives from within the ecumenical movement than by standing on the sidelines.

THE WORLD COUNCIL OF CHURCHES

With the exception of the Roman Catholics, all the main churches and denominations of the world have become members of the WCC. These include not just the great Orthodox churches but also many Pentecostal churches. Theologically the WCC is a tremendous mixture, and thanks to the involvement of Baptists and others, evangelicals within it are becoming increasingly influential.

At the first assembly of the WCC the following resolution was passed:

> The WCC is composed of churches which acknowledge Jesus Christ as God and Saviour. They find their unity in Him. They do not have to create their unity; it is the gift of God. But they know that it is their duty to make common cause in the search for the expression of that unity in work and life.

This is an important statement: the churches and denominations in membership with the WCC recognise that spiritually they are already 'all one in Christ Jesus', but this unity needs to find greater expression. Spiritual realities must be given embodiment in this world if they are to count for anything. How is the world going to believe if it sees the church divided into thousands of different and differing groupings?

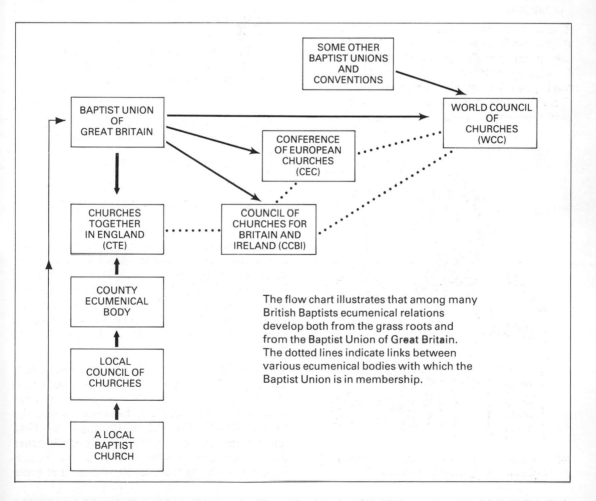

The flow chart illustrates that among many British Baptists ecumenical relations develop both from the grass roots and from the Baptist Union of Great Britain. The dotted lines indicate links between various ecumenical bodies with which the Baptist Union is in membership.

In 1961 at the New Delhi Assembly the WCC sharpened up its basis of belief into the present form:

> The WCC is a fellowship of churches which confess the Lord Jesus Christ as God and Saviour according to the Scriptures, and therefore seeks to fulfil together their common calling to the glory of the one God, Father, Son and Holy Spirit.

It is important to note that this basis includes:

- confession of the Lord Jesus Christ as God and Saviour
- commitment to the Scriptures
- stress on the Trinity

Although reduced to such a minimum, this basis of faith does include three vital statements, the implications of which are major.

TO THINK ABOUT . . .

Should the priority of making common cause in mission override differences over doctrine?

In what ways do Baptists already set aside matters of denominational identity in order to unite with other Christians in evangelism and other aspects of mission?

Are there limits to such co-operation?

THE BRITISH INTER-CHURCH PROCESS

In the United Kingdom the ecumenical movement took a significant step forward in the 1980s with the formal entry of the Roman Catholics into the new ecumenical 'instruments'. This Roman Catholic presence has given concern to many Baptists. The Scottish Baptists, for instance, who had been members of the British Council of Churches, decided that they could no longer be full members of the new Council of Churches for Britain and Ireland, nor of the new Scottish ecumenical body, Action of Churches Together in Scotland. The situation in Wales is somewhat complicated – some churches are anxious to be members of 'Cytûn' ('Together': i.e Churches Together in Wales), but others are not. The Baptist Union of Great Britain has become a member both of CCBI and also of Churches Together in England (CTE).

The Baptist Union of Great Britain has been criticised for its commitment to the inter-church process. One critic, for instance, declared that the Baptist Union:

> has accorded official recognition to the pagan system of Rome with its blasphemous teaching of the mass, its worship and veneration of Mary, the intercession of the saints, and its rejection of 'sola Scriptura', its salvation by works, its superstition and its idolatry.

Such criticism is neither fair nor true. It does not recognise the great changes that have taken place among Roman Catholics since Vatican II in the early 1960s; nor does it recognise that Baptists in co-operating with Roman Catholics are not thereby passing over those fundamental differences which still divide.

The differences between English Roman Catholics and Baptists are not always as great as are imagined – indeed, sometimes the differences between Roman Catholics and Baptists are less than between Baptists and Christians from other traditions. An increasing number of Roman Catholics seek to be biblical Christians, in the sense that they are keen to study God's Word and to treat it as authoritative, not least with regard to some of today's ethical challenges.

Again, an increasing number of Roman Catholics are concerned for mission and evangelism, and are aware that the 'lost' are to be found not only outside their church but also amongst many nominal baptised Catholics who are within their church. Time and again in ecumenical gatherings Baptists and other evangelical Christians discover that they have much in common with those from whom they may have thought they were most distant.

There are, of course, still many things which divide. Furthermore, we have to recognise that while Baptists may find they have much in common with some Roman Catholics, there are other Roman Catholics who appear to live still in a pre-Vatican II world and who have little room for Christians of other traditions. However, truth demands that we recognise that there are things which bind us together in Christ.

In our discussion on relationships between Baptists and Roman Catholics, the focus has been very much on the English scene. It needs to be recognised, however, that there are major differences between English Roman Catholics and Roman Catholic groupings elsewhere. The fact that English Roman Catholics, although a sizeable force, have never formed a majority religious grouping is significant. Indeed, like Baptists, in times past they too have experienced persecution and discrimination. This does make a difference to how they relate to other churches. It may not always be possible, therefore, for Baptists in other parts of the world to be as positive toward Roman Catholics as many English Baptists can be.

English Baptists have also become members of Churches Together in England (CTE), as well as of the larger Council of Churches for Britain and Ireland. CTE's basis and declaration of principle reads as follows:

> CTE unites in pilgrimage those churches in England which, acknowledging God's revelation in Christ, confess the Lord Jesus Christ as God and Saviour according to the Scriptures; and in obedience to God's will and in the power of the Holy Spirit commit themselves
>
> – to seek a deepening of their communion with Christ and with one another in the Church, which is his body, and
> – to fulfil their mission to proclaim the Gospel by common witness and service in the world
>
> to the glory of the one God, Father, Son and Holy Spirit.

BAPTISTS AND EVANGELICALS

Baptist association with other Christians goes far beyond those churches and denominations involved in the ecumenical process. As the most evangelical of mainline denominations, Baptists form a natural bridge to the wider world of evangelical denominations and parachurches which for the time being do not feel able to be part of the ecumenical movement. A large number of Baptist churches, for instance, belong to the Evangelical Alliance, the umbrella under which many of these groups work. Indeed, the mission department of the Baptist Union of Great Britain is a member of the Evangelical Alliance. Baptists are to the fore in such major evangelical gatherings as Spring Harvest and the Keswick Convention. They are also actively involved in many evangelical parachurch organisations, such as Scripture Union and the Universities and Colleges Christian Fellowship.

However, Baptists – in the Baptist Union of Great Britain at least – do not feel it right to limit their fellowship to like-minded evangelicals, but rather seek to associate with all God's people. In the words of the 1965 Baptist Union report on Baptists and Unity:

> Christian unity is of great importance, urgency, and complexity; whilst there is an undeniable spiritual unity binding together all believers to our Lord Jesus Christ and to one another, this needs to be given visible expression in a clearer and more unmistakeable manner than at present.

7

Serving One Another

– a Baptist concept of ministry –

From their beginnings Baptists have treasured the Reformation principle of the 'priesthood of all believers': not for them a clerical hierarchy. Baptists believe that all God's people have equal access to God and in turn have equal responsibility to serve God. While there are differences in role, in terms of status all God's people stand on the same footing before God. Taken seriously, such a doctrine has radical implications for the 'ministry' in which all God's people are involved.

The English words 'ministry' and 'minister' are derived from the Latin for 'service' and 'servant'. Thus we can argue that if all God's people are called to 'serve', then by definition every Baptist (as indeed every Christian) is a 'minister'. Interestingly, the Greek words for 'ministry' and 'minister' are diakonia and diakonos: we might therefore also argue that every Baptist is called to be a deacon. In fact, it is more helpful to see the meaning of diakonia and diakonos pointing to the servant nature of the church: the role of its appointed 'ministers' or 'servants' is to lead the congregation in its varied tasks of Christian 'service'.

British Baptists tend to call their pastors 'ministers'. Although many are happy with this title, we could argue that its use in this special-ised sense implies a denial of the ministry of all God's people. In other countries more functional terms like 'pastor' or 'preacher' are more common. However, at the end of the day titles are unimportant. It is rather the underlying principle which is important: all God's people are called and gifted for service.

> **TO THINK ABOUT . . .**
> Do you agree with the author that at the end of the day titles are unimportant?

THE MINISTRY OF ALL GOD'S PEOPLE

MINISTRY WITHIN THE GATHERED COMMUNITY

This doctrine of every-member ministry is based on the New Testament as a whole, but comes to the fore in Ephesians 4:11–12, where Paul writes of the Risen Christ:

> It was he who gave some to be apostles, some to be prophets, some to be evangelists, and some to be pastors and teachers, to prepare God's people for works of service

or as the RSV puts it

> to equip the saints for the work of ministry.

Ministry for Paul is ministry of the whole people of God – it is not confined to apostles, prophets, evangelists, pastors and teachers.

GIFTED FOR MINISTRY

In line with their calling, all God's people are gifted for ministry. This is the teaching of Paul in Romans 12:4–8 and 1 Corinthians 12:4–12, as also of Peter in 1 Peter 4:10–11. For example, Paul prefaces the list of gifts in 1 Corinthians 12:9–10 with the words, 'Now to each one the manifestation of the Spirit is given for the common good (1 Cor 12:7), and concludes 'All these [gifts] are the work of one and the same Spirit, and he gives them to each man just as he determines' (1 Cor 12:11). Gifts are given to all God's people. Strictly speaking, therefore, all God's people are 'charismatic' (i.e 'gifted' – the term comes from the Greek *charisma* = gift). For many Baptists the movement known as 'charismatic renewal' has been a helpful reminder of this fact.

It is this radical belief that all God's people are 'ministers' which underlies the old Baptist custom, again practised in many churches, of following baptism with the laying-on of hands. Here prayer is made that the baptismal candidates be filled afresh with the Spirit of God and thus empowered for service (see Matt 3:16; Acts 1:8; 8:17). Or as the recent Baptist manual on worship puts it:

> Lord, bless these your servants and strengthen them by your Holy Spirit as we commission them for service in the Church and the world in the name of the Lord Jesus Christ (*Patterns and Prayers for Christian Worship*, p103).

For Baptists the church membership roll is – or at least should be – the 'ministry roll' of the church. In the words of the old cliche, we are 'saved to serve'.

> **TO THINK ABOUT . . .**
>
> 'The deepest word that can be spoken about Christian ministry in all its forms is that it is nothing other than the ministry of the risen Lord among and through his people.'
>
> (Bruce Milne)
>
> What do you understand by that statement and what are its practical implications?

MINISTRY IN THE WORLD

Ministry, however, is not confined to the sphere of the church. This is evident in the prayer quoted above which speaks of 'service in the Church and the world'. Baptists, influenced first by pietism and more recently by charismatic renewal , have sometimes been unduly inward-looking. The temptation for many Baptist pastors has been to organise so many activities within the church that there has been little time and space available for service in the wider world. Increasingly Baptists are recognising that

The church's ministry team.

service in the community, even political action, can be valid forms of Christian ministry.

Although most of this chapter is devoted to the Baptist understanding of ministry within the church, it is likely that for most Christians their primary sphere of service is not in the church but rather within the wider world. This should not be forgotten as we explore the more church centred dimensions to ministry.

> **TO THINK ABOUT . . .**
>
> **'Baptism is the believer's ordination to ministry.'**
>
> **How may that statement help you understand baptism as a sign of your commitment to serve Christ and be his ambassador in every part of life?**

LEADERSHIP: THE MINISTRY OF SOME

THE BIBLICAL BASIS

All God's people are called to serve, but not all are called to lead. As Paul so delightfully makes clear in 1 Corinthians 12, God gives many and various gifts. 'If they were all one part, where would the body be? As it is, there are many parts, but one body' (1 Cor 12:19–20). Most of God's gifts relate to ministry in general. Some, however, relate to the ministry of leadership in particular.

Thus in 1 Corinthians 12:28 Paul refers to 'those with gifts of administration', or as the New RSV more accurately renders, God has given to the church those with gifts of 'leadership'. The underlying Greek noun literally means 'helmsmanship'. It was a term often used metaphorically in Greek literature of the art of government: the statesman guiding the 'ship of state'. Here in 1 Corinthians 12 the ship in question is the church. Within the context of every-member ministry there are those specially gifted to 'preside' over the church, guiding the life of the church in its worship, its mission, and its caring ministry.

This ministry of leadership appears also in the list of the gifts of the Spirit in Romans 12, where Paul writes: 'if it is leadership, let him govern diligently' (Rom 12:8). It is true that in some English versions a somewhat different translation is found: for instance, the RSV translates the phrase, 'he who gives aid, with zeal'. In fact, the underlying Greek verb can mean both 'to lead' and 'to care for'. However, rather than seeking to make distinctions between these two meanings, it is more helpful to note how the two

meanings may interrelate: leadership within a church context is not about the exercise of power but rather about the exercise of care.

The concept of leadership is also present in Paul's third list of spiritual gifts in Ephesians 4:7–13, where amongst the various 'offices' of ministry is found that of the pastor-teacher. Like all the other offices mentioned here, in the first place the emphasis is upon the 'enabling' aspect of this ministry – pastor-teachers enable the people of God to fulfil their various ministries. However, the actual term 'pastor' also carried clear overtones of leadership, for in the ancient world the word 'pastor' or 'shepherd' was often used as a synonym for a 'leader' or 'king'.

A BAPTIST PERSPECTIVE

Baptists have always recognised the need for leadership in the church. As the *Particular Baptist Confession* of 1644 put it:

> every church has power given them from Christ for their better well being, to choose to themselves meet persons into the office of pastors, teachers, elders, deacons . . .

Although the actual terms 'leader' and 'leadership' are not found in earlier Baptist usage, the underlying concept is present in all streams of Baptist life. The various 'offices' of ministry imply leadership.

Not all Baptists are happy with this emphasis on leadership. In particular some would prefer to interpret the role of ordained ministry first and foremost with reference to the 'ministry of Word and Sacrament'. However, as we shall see when we come to examine the role of the pastor, the New Testament basis for such an understanding is questionable. Baptists, if they are true to their roots as also to the Scriptures, are called to be radical believers.

TO THINK ABOUT . . .

Do you agree that the author's emphasis on the term 'leader' is more biblical and helpful for Baptists today than the term 'minister'?

Why do you answer one way or the other?

WOMEN IN LEADERSHIP

Are all the 'offices' of ministry open to women as well as men? Is it true that 'Leadership is male', as one Baptist has recently argued, or are leadership gifts given to both men and women?

The Scriptures teach that the Spirit gives his gifts irrespective of gender (Acts 2:17–18). Although certain cultural situations might limit leadership to men (see 1 Cor 11:3–16; 14:33–36; 1 Tim 2:11–15), in principle there is no Scriptural reason why women should not share in leadership.

In the church in Rome, for instance, women as well as men took the lead: thus Paul mentions that Phoebe was a deacon (Rom 16:1–2), Prisca was a teacher (Rom 16:3), and Junia was even an apostle (see Rom 16:7. Unfortunately the NIV speaks of Junias, rather than Junia: however modern scholarly commentators are unanimous that a woman and not a man is in view). From Acts 21:9 (see also Acts 2:17–18) we learn that women were also prophets.

There is therefore no reason why women may not share the leadership with men in today's church. The long presumed superiority of male over against female no longer exists in Christ (Gal 3:28). In him a new order has come into being. Women can and should expect to play varying roles within Christian leadership.

Baptists, alas, divide over this issue. Although in most Baptist churches women can be – and often are – deacons, in many countries women still cannot be pastors. In the Baptist Union of Great Britain the first woman pastor was recognised in

' . . . and we have complete confidence in the ministry of our sister.'

1922. The then General Secretary of the Baptist Union, J.H. Shakespeare, wrote:

> I regard the liberation of women from the bonds of prejudice . . . as the most helpful feature of our time. Only at its peril can the Church make itself the last ditch of prejudice in this respect or forget that its problems will best be solved by men and women working together.

Yet in spite of the Baptist Union's recognition of women in pastoral ministry, in comparison with other denominations in England, Baptists currently have one of the smallest percentages of female ministers: a recent survey revealed that only eighty (3%) of the 2900 Baptist ministers are women. This compares with nine per cent of Methodist ministers who are women. In Sweden almost half the Baptist ministers, including their present General Secretary, are women.

TO THINK ABOUT . . .

Joan felt increasingly stirred as the sermon went on. Her minister, Bob, was preaching on Romans 12:6–8 and mentioned in the course of his exposition Galatians 3:28. Bob stressed the point that when God bestows a gift, then the recipient of that gift carries responsibility for its exercise.

After the service, Joan waited until Bob was free and then caught his attention. He could see she was concerned about something, so sat with her as she explained her response to his sermon.

'I was especially helped,' she said, 'by your stress on our responsibility to exercise God's gifts to us. Surely then, if Galatians 3:28 is taken seriously, and a woman has gifts of grace, including preaching and leadership, the church has no right to deny her room to exercise those gifts? Also, isn't the woman disobeying God if she fails to exercise them? Why is it then, Bob, that this church so rarely encourages women to exercise gifts of preaching and leadership?'

How would you respond to Joan's questions if it was your church?

THE MINISTRY OF ELDERS AND DEACONS

BAPTIST DIVERSITY

Baptists have expressed their leadership gifts in a variety of ways. John Smyth, the leader of the first English Baptist church in Amsterdam, in his last *Confession of Faith* defined the church as having two sorts of 'ministers':

> Christ hath set in his outward church two sorts of ministers: viz some who are called pastors, teachers, or elders, who administer the word and sacraments, and others, who are called deacons, men and women: whose ministry is to serve tables and wash the saints' feet.

Although the early Baptists envisaged each church having several elders, increasingly the eldership became identified with a one-man-ministry, with the result that most British Baptist churches today have one pastor (the 'elder') and a board (sometimes quaintly called a 'court') of deacons.

There are, however, plenty of exceptions to this pattern. Some Baptist churches have for many years maintained both elders and deacons in addition to having pastors; more recently other churches, which previously only had a pastor and deacons, have as a result of the influence of charismatic renewal reintroduced elders to work alongside their pastors.

Where there are both elders and deacons, then the elders usually have a leadership role in the spiritual and pastoral affairs of the church, while the deacons have responsibility for the more practical aspects of the church's life. Such a distinction between the 'spiritual' and the 'practical' is perhaps open to question. The task of the church treasurer, for instance, is normally seen as a diaconal responsibility, yet the practical business of drawing up a church budget can call for a high degree of spirituality.

NEW TESTAMENT DIVERSITY

In the New Testament we find both elders and deacons. Paul in 1 Timothy 3 lays down the qualities necessary for elders and deacons – unfortunately he says almost next to nothing about their differing duties! There are those who equate the deacons of 1 Timothy 3 with the seven men 'known to be full of the Spirit and wisdom' who in Acts 6:1–6 were chosen 'to wait (διαχονειν – diakonein) on tables'.

But such an equation is highly unlikely. The Seven did not form the kind of management team responsible for matters of church life such as finance, fabric and general administration, which seems to be the role of deacons in churches which have elders and deacons. Rather, they had a key role to play in the pastoral care of the widows of Jerusalem. As Luke develops the story of the church in Acts, it becomes clear that these seven were spiritual leaders of the kind of standing which is normally accorded to elders today: Stephen, for instance,

was a creative theologian (Acts 7), whilst Philip was a gifted evangelist (Acts 8).

It is clear that there was no one blueprint for ministry in New Testament times. The church at Jerusalem was structured differently from the church at Corinth, and almost certainly the church at Corinth was structured differently from the churches addressed in Paul's letter to the Ephesians.

Ultimately what counts are New Testament principles rather than one particular pattern. It is, for instance, more important to release gifts of leadership than to be concerned about particular terminology. With regard to the latter, the present popularity of the term 'elder' in many Baptist churches is open to question. While it was no doubt appropriate in the first century, sociological patterns have changed to such a degree that its current usage is anachronistic. In the first-century world, be it predominantly Greek, Roman or Jewish, people were either 'young' (i.e. under 40) or 'old' (i.e. over 40) – there was no such thing as middle age. Yet in many Baptist churches today there are plenty of middle-aged men who are dignified with the title 'old man' (i.e. elder) – a strange phenomenon indeed!

TO THINK ABOUT . . .

What problems arise from using the New Testament to affirm any one model of ministry?

What varied situations, both in society and in the life of the early church, might have led to different expressions of ministry?

BAPTIST PRINCIPLES CONCERNING LEADERSHIP

Amidst all the diverse patterns of leadership within Baptist churches, there are certain things which are common to all.

LEADERSHIP IS SHARED

In no Baptist church is the pastor the only office-holder. There are always others – deacons and/or elders – who share with the pastor the leadership of the church. In this respect Baptists seek to model their life on the New Testament church, where there was always a plurality of leadership (Acts 13:1; 14:23; 15:23; 20:17, 28; Phil 1:1).

[There are, of course, churches which have no pastor – either because the church is undergoing an 'interregnum', or because it is too small to 'employ' a pastor or does not have a lay pastor. However, the same point applies: leadership is then shared by the deacons and/or elders.]

Traditionally, in a British setting at least, the pastor's right-hand person has been the church secretary, who at times is called upon to represent the interests of the pastor to the church and the interests of the church to the pastor. With the development of elderships, however, in some churches some of the traditional functions of the church secretary have been taken over by the elders, while other tasks are designated to a 'church administrator'. At the end of the day, the precise way in which leadership is shared is unimportant: certainly Scripture is no guide in terms of detail. What is important is that there is shared leadership. Baptists do not conceive the task of a pastor being to 'run' the church on his or her own.

How that task is shared will vary from church to church. In the leaflet *The Ministry of Deacons*, (Baptist Basics Series, published by the Baptist Union of Great Britain), the responsibilities of deacons are defined as the care of the fellowship; leadership in worship and teaching; the care of

the pastor; participation in the deacons' meeting; and leadership in the church meeting.

> **TO THINK ABOUT . . .**
>
> What pattern of shared leadership would best serve the needs, opportunities and mission of your church?
>
> How does that pattern correspond to biblical principles of leadership?

LEADERSHIP IS APPOINTED BY THE CHURCH

Following their understanding of the church meeting, Baptists have given the church the task of appointing elders and deacons. In most British Baptist churches today, for instance, deacons are elected at a church meeting by secret ballot to serve for a period of three years, normally with an option to serve a further term of service. In some churches there is a limit to the number of times a deacon may serve consecutively. In such cases deacons have to take a 'sabbatical' and stand down for a year after, say, two terms of service.

The practice relating to the appointment of elders varies, in that a fixed time limit is not always given. Whether there is a time limit or not, the important point is that elders are appointed by the church and not – as is often the case in other church traditions – by the 'leadership'.

Baptist churches vary over how they publicly recognise those elders and/or deacons whom they elect to leadership. In Britain many Baptist churches today recognise such leadership by appointing deacons and elders with prayer and with the laying-on of hands. Thus *Patterns and Prayers for Christian Worship* (pp168–170) provides an order of service for a 'commissioning of local church workers'.

Among Baptists in the USA, however, it is normal for deacons to be 'ordained' – and for their ordination to be accepted when they move to other churches (however, although ordained for life, most deacons in the States are 'active' for only a limited period and often serve just one term of office).

LEADERSHIP IS ACCOUNTABLE TO THE CHURCH

In a Baptist church elders and/or deacons – as also pastors – may never be a law to themselves. Although the service ('ministry') of elders and deacons is to lead, they are always ultimately subject to the church meeting which in the Baptist understanding of the church, always has the primacy.

THE MINISTRY OF PASTORS

Within the overall context of every-member ministry, and alongside the ministry of deacons and elders, Baptists have also affirmed the ministry of 'pastors'.

In Britain, as elsewhere, there is an increasing tendency for Baptists to follow others in speaking of this particular ministry as 'the ministry'. But as we have already seen, ministry is the duty and responsibility of all God's people. It would be a far healthier witness to the New Testament understanding of the church if Baptists retained the functional term of 'pastor'. True, there are difficulties in such terminology. The term 'pastor', in Britain at least, has often been used of those who have not been formally trained – Baptists have, for instance, talked of 'lay pastors', and used the term 'minister' of 'the professionals'. Furthermore, it could be argued that the term 'pastor' is a hang-over from a rural society, and sounds strange in today's largely urban world. Would the phrase 'pastoral leader' be an improvement?

Although John Smyth argued for a college of pastors in each church, claiming that if a church only has one pastor, then those with pastoral gifts who join it will be wasted, in the average European Baptist church today there is usually only one pastor. Normally only larger churches have more than one pastor. Increasingly, although there may be but one pastor in name (and on the pay-roll), many of the pastoral tasks are shared with other suitably gifted members. The pastor, however, is the one who spearheads the work of the church's mission and ministry, and thereby acts as the leader of the leaders.

TEACHER

How do pastors express leadership in the life of a local church? Paul in Ephesians 4:11 speaks of the risen Christ having given to the church 'some to be pastors and teachers'. The construction of the underlying Greek makes it clear that this is one and the same office: i.e. the chief duty of any pastor is to teach – the flock must be fed. For Baptists this task of preaching and teaching – 'the ministry of the word' (see Acts 6:4; also 1 Tim 3:2; 5:17) – has always been

paramount. Indeed, in the German-speaking world, Baptist pastors have traditionally been called not 'pastors' but 'preachers' (Lehrer).

CARER/SHEPHERD

Along with the teaching role also goes the 'caring' role. The very metaphor 'pastor' (derived from the Latin word meaning 'shepherd') suggests the tending of the flock. Rightly understood, pastoral care involves not just helping the hurting but also encouraging people to grow and develop in the Christian faith. This is the 'episcopal' function of 'oversight' (see Acts 20:28: also 1 Pet 5:2), which may be shared, but never finally delegated.

ENABLER

A further role is indicated by Paul in Ephesians 4:11–12: pastor-teachers are to 'equip the saints for the work of ministry' (RSV). Far from monopolising ministry, the pastor is called to multiply ministry. Baptists along with others have increasingly stressed this 'enabling' aspect of pastoral ministry. Indeed, in a booklet issued

'He put four years of his best sermons on a disk, then accidentally pressed ERASE.'

by the Baptist Union of Great Britain in 1976, it was claimed that 'perhaps the term "enabler" best describes the role of the minister today' (John Nicholson, *Ministry*, p28). Although this is an overstatement, it expresses validly the calling of every Baptist to be a minister.

So far we have sought to define pastoral ministry with the church primarily in view. However, no Baptist pastor worth his or her salt will be unconcerned for the world for whom Christ died (see 2 Tim 4:5). The pastoral task includes mobilising God's people in mission, whether that be evangelism or social action.

Pastoral leadership, then, includes the preaching and teaching of God's Word, the oversight and equipping of God's people, with a view to advancing the Kingdom of God in both word and deed. None of these specific tasks of teaching, pastoral care, evangelism, and enabling, are exclusive to those engaged in pastoral ministry. In any local church it would be exceedingly limiting if, for instance, pastoral care and evangelism were the exclusive preserve of the pastor alone – if a church is to grow and develop, such tasks need to be shared. However, as the overall leader of a church, the pastor is accountable for ensuring that these tasks are responsibly delegated.

ORDINATION

The distinctive nature of pastoral ministry is recognised in the service of ordination, and the enrolment of the ordained on the denomination's list of accredited 'ministers'. In contrast with the locally-recognised ministry of elders and deacons, ordination accords the formal recognition and trust of the wider church to the ordained. This marks the culmination of a lengthy period of testing and training, and is the occasion when churches together publicly recognise certain individuals as called of God to exercise leadership among them. Through the laying-on of hands and prayer, the churches ask that God will fill afresh with his Spirit those who embark upon this new stage of their Christian service (see Acts 6:1–16; 13:1–3; 1 Tim 4:14).

Although in a British Baptist context a service of ordination normally takes place in a local church, Baptists have never regarded ordination as just an act of the local church. Ordination involves national recognition, and so representatives of the local association and the Baptist Union are present.

Elsewhere ordination is handled somewhat differently, but the same principles apply: for example, in Australia ordination is seen in the first place as the responsibility of the state Baptist union, and therefore 'mass'-ordinations take place at their annual assemblies.

Some Baptists have been keen to give even greater significance to ordination. In the eighteenth century Baptists began to take up the Reformed understanding of ordination as a setting aside of a person to 'the ministry of word and sacrament'. In *Patterns and Prayers for Christian Worship* a tendency is found to this sacerdotal or priestly emphasis. But in our judgement at least there are no biblical grounds for such an understanding. Although the 'ministry of the word' is a vital and important part of any pastor's calling, there is nothing in Scripture to indicate that this is an exclusive calling.

Likewise, although in most church situations the pastor will normally share in baptising and preside at the Lord's Table, there is nothing in Scripture to indicate that either ordinance is the pastor's exclusive preserve. Where the pastor baptises or presides at the Lord's Table, the pastor does so, not in virtue of being a priest mediating between God and his people, but in virtue of being the recognised and trusted leader of God's flock. Indeed, Baptists on the whole accept that there is no scriptural reason why anyone may not perform either function provided it is at the invitation of the church.

TO THINK ABOUT . . .

Are the terms 'lay pastor' and 'lay preacher' helpful and appropriate terms to describe the ministry of some who serve in Baptist churches?

If you are uncomfortable with the terms, why are you, and what alternative terms would you suggest for those who exercise that ministry?

THE MINISTRY OF SUPERINTENDENTS

APOSTLES

So far we have looked at pastoral leadership within a local context. However, from the beginning of the church's life there were those who had a wider ministry which went beyond that of the local church. Thus Paul in his list of ministries in Ephesians 4:11 wrote that the risen Christ 'gave some to be apostles, some to be prophets, some to be evangelists, and some to be pastors and teachers'. In the New Testament church pastors and teachers were – for the most part at least – locally based, whereas apostles, prophets and evangelists seem to have exercised a 'translocal ministry' (see Eph 2:20; 3:5; also Rev 22:9).

With regard to the apostles in particular, it is clear from the way the New Testament uses the term 'apostles' that it refers not just to the Twelve, that unrepeatable and unique group who were witnesses to the resurrection of Jesus (Acts 1:21–22), but to a broader group of men and women who were given a roving commission in the life of the church. Thus the term 'apostle' is used of James (1 Cor 15:7), Barnabas (Acts 14:3–4, 14; 1 Cor 9:5–6), Silas and Timothy (1 Thess 1:1, 2:7), Andronicus and Junia (Rom 16:7). The word 'apostle' literally means 'one who is sent'; these 'apostles' were sent out from a church or group of churches with an evangelistic and overseeing function which went beyond the local church.

MESSENGERS

This 'apostolic' role was revived by General Baptists in the seventeenth century when they created the office of 'Messenger' (a term so similar to that of 'apostle' that some modern versions of the Bible use it as a synonym for 'apostle'). These messengers had a specific ministry beyond the local church. In the first place they had the responsibility of evangelism and church planting, and of caring for the newly formed churches. They also were sometimes called in to give advice and counsel to one or more of the churches who had originally appointed them.

In course of time the office of messenger died out in Baptist churches, but in 1916 the Baptist Union of Great Britain created ten 'General Superintendents' whose task was to care for the pastors and churches in the ten geographical 'Areas' into which the country was divided. In some respects this new office was seen as a return to the office of messenger.

SUPERINTENDENTS

Superintendents today, however, are for the most part chosen more for their pastoral than their evangelistic qualities. Indeed, the very term 'superintendent' lacks the dynamism of the old term 'messenger'; it suggests maintenance (a not unimportant task) rather than mission. Therefore some associations have appointed 'missioners' to work alongside their superintendent. On the other hand, some superintendents would like – in theory at least – to see their primary role as missionary strategists.

> **TO THINK ABOUT . . .**
> **What title do you support for those whom the churches set apart to exercise wider ministry in the association and area?**
>
> **What in your view should be a 'superintendent's' primary tasks?**

The Baptist Union of Great Britain currently defines the work of the General Superintendents as follows:

- to give pastoral care to ministers and their families;
- to give pastoral oversight to the churches, encouraging and advising them in their mission;
- to provide leadership in the Area in taking initiatives for the furtherance of Christian witness and education;
- to facilitate ministerial settlement;
- to act as the representative of the Baptist

Union at the appropriate level in ecumenical discussion and action;

- generally to promote the objects of the Union.

BAPTIST BISHOPS?

In this increasingly ecumenical age there are those who liken superintendents to bishops. Certainly there are similarities in role, but there are also distinct differences caused not least by the Baptist understanding of the local church as having 'liberty, under the guidance of the Holy Spirit, to interpret and administer His [Jesus Christ's] Laws'. In spite of their name, in their dealings with local churches, superintendents do not have more than moral and persuasive authority. In the words of a former Baptist college principal, 'they are encouragers and advisers' (H. Wheeler Robinson). Therefore, in their dealings with other denominations, superintendents may represent the Baptist Union, but at the end of the day they cannot commit Baptist churches to any particular policy.

However, the most important reason for not referring to superintendents as Baptist 'bishops' is found in the unhelpful associations connected with the Anglican and Roman Catholic doctrine of the 'historic episcopate'. The 'historic episcopate' has been defined by the Church of England as 'not merely a method of Church government (in which sense it would hardly be called historic)', but 'a distinct, substantive and historic transmission of the commission of the apostles in and by which our Lord formed his disciples into a distinctly organised body or Church'. On this understanding of episcopacy, the bishops stand in 'apostolic succession' and thus are held to be of the very essence of the church. The bishops not only safeguard the faith of the church, but in their very selves represent the continuity and unity of the church. Without episcopal ordination, any form of ordained ministry is in fact 'invalid' and has no authority.

This understanding of episcopacy is a direct denial of the Baptist understanding of the church. As we have seen, the church is the people of God and cannot be summed up in particular individuals. When, for instance, Baptist pastors or superintendents are called to represent the local or wider church, they do so always on behalf of the local or wider church and not because, as a result of the laying-on of hands, they in themselves provide a focus of the church's unity. Furthermore, not only is this doctrine of apostolic succession untenable on historical grounds – there has not been an unbroken succession of bishops – it is also not scriptural. Indeed, if the doctrine of apostolic succession is found in Scripture at all, then it relates to the faithful transmission of the Word (2 Tim 2:2) rather than to who lays hands on whom.

> **TO THINK ABOUT . . .**
>
> **Does the author persuade you of the case against Baptist bishops?**
>
> **If we expect superintendents to give strong leadership, must we vest in them more power and authority than we do at present?**

Because of all these associations, realism dictates that, within a British context at least, the word 'bishop' can never become a functional term. There is no case for Baptists using the term 'bishop' of their superintendents. Indeed, if there were a case at all for Baptists reviving the New Testament office of bishop, then in the first place it would need to be applied to the office of pastor – for in the New Testament the office of bishop belonged to local rather than trans-local ministry.

If British Baptists wish to find an alternative term to 'superintendent', then perhaps they need to look beyond their own shores. In Germany, for instance, Baptists call the person executing superintendency functions 'the association leader'. In the United States associational officers are sometimes called 'executive secretaries' or 'directors of mission'. Whatever the name, what ultimately counts is that a lead is given in mission and ministry to the churches and pastors of the associations.

OTHER TRANSLOCAL MINISTRIES

In addition to superintendents, Baptists have developed a wide range of other 'translocal' ministries. Into this category come such people as union or convention officials, college principals and tutors, association missioners and ministers. Although there may be no strict New Testament precedent for their respective offices, the principle at least is found in the translocal ministry of the apostles, prophets and evangelists.

> **TO THINK ABOUT . . .**
>
> **Should Baptists be glad to see these 'translocal' ministries expand? What forms of such ministry are needed to meet the challenges and opportunities of the 1990's?**
>
> **Do those in translocal ministry unhelpfully draw resources away from the heart of the Baptist understanding of the church, namely the life, ministry and mission of the local church?**

SUMMARY

Baptists delight in the many and varied gifts of the Spirit that God has given to all his people for 'ministry'. They happily acknowledge that amidst this diversity there is a variety of roles. They have no difficulty in recognising the need for full-time Christian service, and have encouraged the development of 'professional' pastoral ministry and other specialised forms of Christian ministry. They reject, however, any false division between 'clergy' and 'laity'. They believe passionately that all God's people are called to Christian ministry – for them the 'priesthood of all believers' is foundational. Here again we discover that Baptists are radical believers.

8
Sharing the Faith
– Baptists engage in mission –

BAPTISTS ARE A MISSIONARY PEOPLE

IN PRINCIPLE

It was Gerhard Oncken, the great pioneer of Baptist work on the European Continent, who coined the slogan, 'Every Baptist a missionary'. Although we cannot pretend that Baptists have always lived up to their missionary calling, they have been characterised by a passion for the gospel. Indeed, their rite of believers' baptism emphasises the necessity of conversion.

Not surprisingly, evangelistic activity dominates the life of many Baptist churches. Guest services, evangelistic coffee mornings, visitation evangelism, mini-missions of one kind or another – all these activities, and many more, are typical of an average Baptist church.

It is no accident that William Carey, the pioneer of the modern missionary movement, and Billy Graham, the world's best known evangelist, are Baptists. They are simply the tip of an iceberg. The Baptist historian, W.T. Whitley, noted that of the fifteen men who signed the *Particular Baptist Confession* in 1644, 'every one who can be traced was an ardent evangelist'. John Bunyan was converted as a result of a group of Baptist washer-women gossiping the gospel. Evangelism is part of the Baptist way of life.

It is significant that in the relatively brief 'declaration of principle' adopted by the Baptist Union of Great Britain as its basis of union, the third and final principle declares:

> it is the duty of every disciple to bear personal witness to the Gospel of Jesus Christ, and to take part in the evangelisation of the world.

IN PRACTICE

This principle of union is reflected in the life of Baptist churches in general. Thus most Baptist churches will from time to time provide faith-sharing courses whereby members are helped to

> always be prepared to give an answer to everyone who asks you to give the reason for the hope you have (1 Pet 3:15).

Most Baptist churches also have many groups, for young people, for women, and for men, which in principle at least are evangelistic in orientation.

Baptist churches are sometimes in danger of so over-organising evangelism that their members do not have sufficient time to develop relationships with their neighbours and colleagues at work. This in turn means that there are very few occasions for meaningful and effective evangelism. The hustle and bustle of life in an average Baptist church is reflected not too unfairly in the ditty:

> Mary had a little lamb,
> She also had a sheep.
> And then they joined the Baptist church
> And died through lack of sleep.

Baptists may sometimes, therefore, be unwise in the way they organise their life together. And yet, for all the criticisms they may at times justly deserve, their passion for evangelism is undoubted.

This commitment to evangelism is common to all Baptists everywhere. For example, an illustration of such commitment is provided by the churches in the Southern Baptist Convention in the United States (the largest Baptist grouping in the world), whose Sunday services almost

---

TO THINK ABOUT . . .

Liz, a nurse, had taken as much as she could put up with. The church meeting was considering yet another programme of evangelism. She knew the right thing was to get to her feet and share her frustration – no good bottling it up.

'Pastor,' she began, rather nervously, 'I don't know if I'm alone, but my heart sinks at schemes for evangelism which take up hours of time in discussion, planning and then carrying out.'

Liz warmed to her theme.

'I desperately need help and support in witnessing for Jesus by the kind of person I am day by day at the hospital and among my neighbours and friends. What was it the visiting preacher said the other Sunday: "Lifestyle evangelism is the most effective form of evangelism".'

There were several murmurs of approval from around the room.

Was Liz being fair to 'programmes of evangelism'?

What contribution would you make to the discussion started by Liz?

---

always conclude with an 'altar call', i.e. an appeal to members of the congregation to come to the front of the church as a token of their desire to hand over their lives to Christ. While such a regular extension of an appeal is foreign to British Baptists, even in Britain it is customary in most churches to give an 'appeal' at baptismal services, as well as on other occasions.

A further sign of Baptist commitment to evangelism is the way in which every Baptist World Alliance Congress ends with an evangelistic meeting. Indeed the 1990 Congress of the Baptist World Alliance enthusiastically adopted the so-called Seoul Covenant, and in this way sought to commit the world-wide family of Baptists to a decade of mission.

'No Pastor, not 198 people! We saved £198 using Bubble and Squeak Caterers.'

THE SEOUL COVENANT

We dedicate ourselves anew to the task of world evangelisation with the aim that by AD 2000 every person will have the opportunity to respond to the message of God's love in Jesus Christ in an authentic and meaningful way.

We call upon Baptists, collectively and individually, around the world to join in this covenant:

To this end:

1. We confess that the mission in which we engage belongs to God. It is our joy and responsibility, inspired by the Holy Spirit, to be witnesses throughout the world to Jesus Christ, our crucified and risen Lord.

2. Since Baptists are part of the whole family of God, such witness calls us to pray and work with other Christians in this vital task.

3. Because all people stand under the judgement of God, the gospel of salvation needs to be proclaimed and demonstrated to every generation until Jesus Christ returns. We do this humbly, for we are all sinners saved by grace, yet confidently, for it is the power of God by which people are saved.

4. Believing that personal faith in Jesus Christ involves commitment to his body, the church, we aim to build communities that will be effective signs of God's kingdom in the world.

5. We confess that inherent within the gospel is the need for God's people to work for a world where peace and justice are pursued, and whose environment is preserved.

6. As members of the Baptist family, we pledge ourselves to sacrificial giving for this purpose, and to provide resources to enable all to share the good news of salvation in their own cultures and languages.

7. Jesus Christ is the hope of the world. He is the centre around which our lives revolve. He is the sovereign presence in the kingdom in which we live and work. His truth is eternal, his love unchanging, his grace sufficient. To him we commit our lives totally, joyfully, unreservedly.

To God be the glory.

TO THINK ABOUT . . .
What does the Seoul Covenant tell us about a Baptist understanding of mission?

MISSION INCLUDES BOTH EVANGELISM AND SOCIAL ACTION

Traditionally Baptists have highlighted the Great Commission of Matthew 28:18–20 as their basis for mission. There the risen Lord Jesus declares:

> All authority in heaven and on earth has been given to me. Therefore go and make disciples of all nations, baptising them in the name of the Father and of the Son and of the Holy Spirit, and teaching them to obey everything I have commanded you. And surely I will be with you always, to the very end of the age.

LAUSANNE 1974

Sometimes Baptists have interpreted the Great Commission in terms of a rather narrow evangelism, but in recent years a more holistic understanding of mission has again emerged, twinning social action with evangelism. The primary impetus for this re-evaluation of mission came from the International Congress on World Evangelisation held at Lausanne in 1974, out of which came the Lausanne Covenant. This affirmed that 'evangelism and socio-political involvement are both part of our Christian duty. In the church's mission of sacrificial service evangelism is primary', but such evangelism, it was recognised, must take place in the context of a 'deep and costly penetration of the world'.

In one sense there was nothing new about this insight. There have always been Baptists who have held a concept of mission broad enough to encompass both evangelism and social action. For instance, in the nineteenth century C.H. Spurgeon, alongside his vigorous evangelism and his church planting activities, founded an orphanage for children and to his cost protested against the American slave trade. However, in reaction to a 'liberal protestantism', which at the beginning of the twentieth century had sometimes expressed itself in an anaemic social gospel, many Baptists over-reacted and turned their backs entirely on the social implications of the gospel. The Lausanne Congress helped evangelical Christians – Baptists included – to recover their heritage.

GRAND RAPIDS 1982

In a follow-up conference at Grand Rapids, the Lausanne Continuing Committee issued a report, *Evangelism and Social Responsibility*, which distinguished between social service and social action. See the chart below.

The Grand Rapids report raised the question: 'Does social action belong to the church as a church, or is it the prerogative of individual believers who make up the church, and of groups?' Baptists, like the authors of the report, are divided in their answers to this question.

THE NAZARETH MANIFESTO

With the claims of social action in mind, attention is now often drawn to the Nazareth manifesto of Luke 4:18–19 as, in part at least, a description of the church's mission:

> The Spirit of the Lord is on me,
> because he has anointed me
> to preach good news to the poor.
> He has sent me to proclaim freedom for the prisoners
> and recovery of sight for the blind,

Social Service	Social action
Relieving human need	Removing the causes of human need
Philanthropic activity	Political and economic activity
Seeking to minister to individuals and families	Seeking to transform the structures of society
Works of mercy	The quest for justice

to release the oppressed,
to proclaim the year of the Lord's favour.

Some argue, particularly those involved in urban mission, that this Nazareth manifesto should be combined with the resurrection mandate of Matthew 28. Thus Colin Marchant, a former President of the Baptist Union of Great Britain, and for many years committed to mission in East London, declares:

> Too often it has been an 'either . . . or'; either social justice or personal conversion. The great need has been to hold both together. The two streams will then flow into the key model of 1 Corinthians 12 – the Body of Christ uniting believers in a total ministry of directed love towards the world in its anguish and yearning.

This new emphasis on a broader understanding of mission is a reflection of our calling to be both light and salt in the world (Matt 5:13–16). In the darkness of this world we are to point to Jesus, the light of the world; indeed we are to let his light shine through us. Also, where the world is rotting and decaying, we are to hold putrefaction at bay by getting involved in the world's structures, actively pursuing peace and justice in our society.

TO THINK ABOUT . . .

How does your church set about mobilising its members to fulfil both the Great Commission and the Nazareth Manifesto?

What part do you play in their fulfilment?

INTEGRATING THREE DIMENSIONS

Murray Robertson, senior pastor of Spreydon Baptist Church, Christchurch, New Zealand, concluded his reflections on more than twenty years of ministry, in which his church grew from fifty to over 1200 members, in the following words:

> So the journey has involved the integration of three dimensions. They complement each other. Without a heart for the poor and needy those involved in the charismatic dimension of the faith can often end up with a shallow triumphalism. Yet the charismatic dimension can bring an experience of spiritual vitality that can be lacking with those involved in the struggle for justice. Together the charismatic and justice dimensions form a potent mix for evangelism.

EVANGELISM AND CHURCH GROWTH

A POST-CHRISTIAN SOCIETY

A broader concept of mission does not lessen the need to 'make disciples'. The Great Commission of Jesus is as imperative as ever. Indeed, with an increasingly non-churchgoing society the Great Commission becomes even more imperative for the church in Europe.

The church in Britain, as in Europe in general, faces a missionary task of the first order – but it is a missionary task with a difference, for the world in which we live is a post-Christian world. Alan Gilbert, an Australian sociologist, defines our society in these terms:

> A post-Christian society is not one from which Christianity has departed, but one in which it has

become marginal. It is a society where to be irreligious is to be normal, where to think and act in secular terms is to be conventional, where neither status nor respectability depends upon the practice or profession of religious faith.

Some members of such a society continue to find Christianity a profound, vital influence in their lives, but in so doing they place themselves outside the mainstream of social life and culture. Like the early Christians in a pre-Christian, classical world, they become a 'peculiar people', anomalous in their primary beliefs, assumptions, values and norms, distinctive in important aspects of outlook and behaviour. They become a sub-culture.

TO THINK ABOUT . . .

'Most outreaches turn out to be inreaches.'

From your experience of evangelism in Baptist churches, is there any truth in that caricature? How do you explain that tendency?

A SUPERMARKET OF BELIEFS

We live in a world where the Christian faith is one of a number of options. In the past, maybe, our churches were in competition with others – the choice was perhaps between being an Anglican, a Roman Catholic, a Baptist, or whatever. But today we are in competition with a much vaster range of faiths and non-faiths. We live in a supermarket of beliefs.

The first step in effective evangelism is to recognise the range of beliefs outside the Christian church. There are not simply the saved and the unsaved – there is wide variety among the unsaved:

- those on the near fringe of the church who are known to us by name;
- nominal Christians on the far fringe of the church who only darken the door of the church for christenings, weddings and funerals;
- 'neo-pagans' who have given up Christianity altogether, but give evidence in various ways that they are still conscious of a supernatural dimension to life;
- followers of other main-line religions such as Hindus, Jews, Muslims, and Sikhs;
- the truly 'secularised', who for all intents and purposes live in a world totally closed off from God.

TO THINK ABOUT . . .

Does this way of identifying various groups in your community help distinguish varied strategies you need to adopt for commending Christ and the gospel to those different groups?

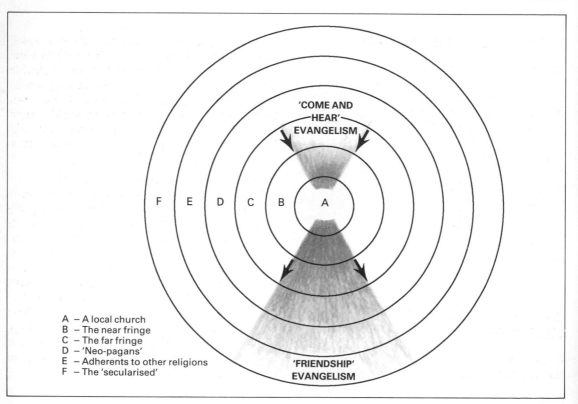

A – A local church
B – The near fringe
C – The far fringe
D – 'Neo-pagans'
E – Adherents to other religions
F – The 'secularised'

'We think we may have hit on a very unusual but fruitful means of evangelism.'

EFFECTIVE STRATEGIES

The second step in effective evangelism is to develop a wide range of strategies appropriate to these various groups. Unfortunately too much evangelism presumes that people are nearer the Kingdom of God than they actually are. Traditional evangelism, with its emphasis on 'come and hear' gets little further than those on the 'near fringe'. A new way of thinking is necessary, which involves Christians in the costly business of bridge-building. Evangelistic programmes are limited in their effectiveness. What is called for is 'friendship evangelism', otherwise known as 'life-style' or 'incarnational' evangelism, whereby Christ is seen in and through his people.

BAPTISTS AND CHURCH GROWTH

It was from a desire for effective evangelism that the modern church growth movement deve-loped. Initially the proponents of church growth had the needs of the two-thirds world in view, but in the 1970s their insights were applied to the USA in the first place (by, among others, British church leaders like Eddie Gibbs), and then to other parts of the Western world. British Baptists, such as Tom Houston and Roy Pointer, played a key role in the domestication of these insights in the United Kingdom.

One of the concerns of the church growth movement, which Baptists have generally welcomed, has been its emphasis on making disciples. Whereas traditional crusade evangelism has emphasised making decisions for Christ, the church growth movement has promoted 'body evangelism', i.e. the kind of evangelism which brings people into the Body of Christ. This is the kind of evangelism presupposed in the Great Commission of Matthew 28, where Jesus commanded us to 'make disciples, baptising them . . . teaching them . . .' This kind of evangelism fits well with the Baptist concept of the believers' church.

BIRDS OF A FEATHER . . .

One of the more controversial aspects of the church growth movement has been its development of the 'homogeneous unit' as an evangelistic tool. A homogeneous unit is 'a section of society in which all the members have some characteristic in common – a segment of society whose common characteristic is a culture or a language'. Church growth thinkers have argued that churches composed of basically one kind of people are more likely to grow – for 'birds of a feather flock together'.

Donald McGavran, the father of the modern church growth movement, observed that 'people like to become Christians without crossing racial, linguistic or class barriers'. Baptists in many of the large cities in the world have used this insight to establish churches targeted at particular ethnic groups.

Not everybody has welcomed this use of the homogeneous principle, arguing that Galatians 3:28 teaches the principle of cultural diversity within the church of God. Others have argued for a middle way, whereby evangelistic groups are set up to target people of a particular age, class or race, but once these people are won to Christ they are then integrated into heterogeneous churches. The debate continues!

CHURCH PLANTING

Church growth is not simply about 'bigger and better churches'. From the start the church growth movement has been concerned for the effective multiplication of congregations: i.e. church planting is another vital aspect of church growth. Indeed, there are many who maintain that it is only through a vigorous programme of church planting that the world can be won to Christ.

It was out of the conviction that church planting is 'the most effective evangelistic method under heaven' (Peter Wagner) that 250 Baptists from forty-five nations met together at the Swanwick Conference Centre in Derbyshire in March 1992, and as a result produced the 'Derbyshire Declaration' with its call to establish new churches. The final paragraph of their message originally read: 'We invite every Baptist congregation in the world to establish at least one new congregation by 2000 AD.' That would have been a challenge! Point 10 of the final Declaration states the revised challenge.

SOCIAL ACTION AND HUMAN RIGHTS

Mission is not exhausted by evangelism. The Great Commission is presented with a variety of facets in the Gospels. The version in John 20:21 is peculiarly significant: 'As the Father has sent me, I am sending you.' Just as Jesus cared for the poor, the sick, the oppressed, and those on the margins of society, so we must be concerned for all those who are in one way or another deprived.

HUMAN RIGHTS

This social dimension to the gospel has not been neglected by Baptists. They have a proud record of concern for human rights. To mention but a few names, there was Thomas Helwys and his plea for religious toleration; William Carey, who caused the practice of widow-burning ('suttee')

to be outlawed in British India; William Knibb, who brought about the end of slavery in the West Indies; Martin Luther King, whose freedom marches contributed to the ending of segregation in the United States.

TO THINK ABOUT . . .

How may Baptists today express concern for human rights? In particular, what human rights issues in our own society and in your community could your church become involved in?

What are some implications of extending to other minority groups in society the freedom of conscience for which Baptists, among others, have stood and fought?

THE DERBYSHIRE DECLARATION

We, the delegates commit ourselves anew to the task of world evangelism and specifically to the establishment of new churches. We direct the following message to the family of Baptists throughout the world.

1. We give thanks to God that throughout the world there is a mighty movement of the Holy Spirit and in many countries countless new congregations are being established in urban, suburban and rural areas, among various ethnic and sociological groups and in areas where the Gospel has not been previously preached.

2. We believe that a powerful means for growth at the disposal of the Christian Church, and a most effective means to fulfil the Great Commission, is the establishing of new congregations.

3. We resolve to establish churches that enable the character and teaching of Jesus to become incarnate within particular communities.

4. We call on those engaged in new church development to be committed to prayer, creative in thinking, thorough in preparation and innovative in methodology, while always seeking to develop communities of faith consistent with biblical methods, guided by God the Holy Spirit.

5. We challenge Baptist leaders and pastors to use the gifts, skills and enthusiasm of all laity, women, men and young people, in developing new patterns of church planting.

6. We recognise with joy new congregations everywhere that are bringing life and vitality to Baptist unions and conventions. We urge congregations who to date may not have had the joy and stimulus of establishing new congregations to consider prayerfully the call of God to engage in this ministry.

7. We encourage new churches both to disciple and nurture new converts and to inspire their people to maintain a spirit of love in a holistic way to all in need, being witnessing communities that oppose injustice and work for peace.

8. We acknowledge that our preoccupation with the needs of our own areas, including establishing new churches, may blind us to the urgent need to proclaim and demonstrate the Gospel in areas of the world which have not heard of the love of God in Jesus Christ and realise that churches need to be planted in these unevangelised regions.

9. We commit ourselves to promote new church planting so that more and more people gain the opportunity of hearing the Good News of God in Jesus Christ.

10. We invite every Baptist congregation in the world to establish, or to explore the possibility of joining with other churches in establishing, at least one new congregation by 2000 AD.

TO THINK ABOUT . . .
How will you and your church respond to this 'message to the Baptist family . . .'?

SOCIAL ACTION

Baptists, however, have not simply protested. They have also expressed their social concern through a wide variety of service agencies – ranging from hospitals to schools, homes for the mentally handicapped and provision of sheltered housing for the elderly. Initially this activity was independent of the state. However, as governments have developed their own social agencies, Baptists have increasingly co-operated with the state.

State involvement in the provision of social services is to be welcomed. It can, however, lead to problems as far as a distinctively Christian contribution to society is concerned. For instance, at one stage British Baptists had their own order of deaconesses, who to a large extent fulfilled the role of social workers helping the poor and underprivileged. This order of deaconesses no longer exists – their work has been taken over by the state. There are, of course, plenty of Baptists working as social workers – but not now under a Baptist aegis.

The story of the British Baptist contribution to the world of education is somewhat similar: at one stage in different parts of the country Baptists used to run their own schools or support the British Schools which provided an alternative to the Anglican National Schools. With the provision of universal education by the state, most Baptists felt it right to support the state sector, with the result that until very recently there were no distinctively Baptist schools left in Britain. Recently, however, a few Baptist churches have started up their own 'Christian' schools to counteract what they perceive as increasingly secular trends in education.

A CHRISTIAN CONTRIBUTION

The question, therefore, which faces Baptist churches in Britain and elsewhere is this: to what extent is a distinctively Baptist or Christian contribution called for in the area of social need and concern? There is, of course, no one answer. Christians are needed to work within the state sector. On the other hand, the state's provision will never be sufficient: voluntary agencies to complement the work of the statutory agencies will always be needed. Furthermore, there will always be the need for a distinctively Christian contribution – not least in Christians acting as a social conscience to the local community and to the nation.

> **TO THINK ABOUT . . .**
> How do you react to the argument that Christians should put their energies into working for better state response to social need, rather than setting up separate Christian agencies?

MOBILISING THE CHURCH FOR SOCIAL ACTION

At the end of the day each local church should devise its own strategy for social action appropriate to its own community. Such a strategy ought to include the following elements:

CORPORATE PRAYER

In the church's prayers of intercession there are constant opportunities to include world, national, and community concerns. Maybe a special 'ministry team' might be set up to ensure that a wide range of concerns are regularly brought to the attention of the church

SUPPORT FOR 'PROFESSIONALS'

Many churches will have a sprinkling of people professionally involved in community service: e.g. social workers, teachers, policemen and women, prison officers, health visitors, doctors, nurses. These are at the 'sharp' end of life, and may encounter suspicion and misunderstanding, if not hostility, in the course of their work. Such people can benefit from the prayerful support of their local churches.

ENCOURAGEMENT FOR 'VOLUNTEERS'

There are many areas of voluntary service in which Christians can and should be involved: e.g. the magistracy, school-governing boards, parent-teacher associations, health consultative councils, trade unions. It is not enough to leave such involvement to individual initiative. A wise church will encourage suitably gifted people in community service – even if it means less time for formal church activities.

INVOLVEMENT IN POLITICAL PROCESSES

Although no church may align itself with one particular political party, it is important that Christians are involved in politics – both at local and national level. Churches need to encourage members to belong to political parties of varying hue, and in this way act as salt in the world.

LOCAL COMMUNITY PROJECTS

A church not only needs to serve its community through the involvement of its individual members, it also needs to be seen as a church that cares. Projects need to be found which offer both an avenue of Christian service for members and an opportunity for the church to demonstrate in a practical and concrete way the love of God in Christ.

> *TO THINK ABOUT . . .*
>
> **Find out all you can about the work of both the Kaleidoscope Project and the Oasis Trust.**
>
> **In what ways are they expressing Baptist convictions about Christian mission?**

BAPTISTS AND OVERSEAS MISSION

AN IRREPRESSIBLE 'ENTHUSIAST'

At a ministers' meeting in 1785 William Carey raised the question

> whether the command given to the Apostles to teach all nations was not obligatory on all succeeding ministers to the end of the world, seeing that the accompanying promise was of equal extent.

A senior Baptist minister, John Collet Ryland, told him to sit down: 'You're an enthusiast. When God is pleased to convert the heathen, He'll do it without consulting you and me.' But Carey refused to give up. In 1792 he brought out a book of 87 pages entitled, *An Enquiry into the Obligations of Christians, to use means for the conversion of the heathens, in which the religious state of the different nations of the world, the success of former undertakings, and the practicability of further undertakings, are considered.* Carey in this carefully researched work argued for the formation of a missionary society, founded along the lines of a trading company. In 1792, after preaching his 'deathless' sermon at Nottingham, with its great watchword, 'Expect great things; Attempt great things', his fellow Baptists were galvanised into action and in November 1792 the Baptist Missionary Society came into being, with a capital of £13 2s 6d. From that action the beginnings of the modern missionary movement are traced.

> *TO THINK ABOUT . . .*
>
> **'A church should think globally but act locally.'**
>
> **What do you understand by that expression and how may your church meeting apply that principle?**

THE CONTINUING STORY

Needless to say, over the years the missionary enterprise has changed out of all recognition. The pioneering days of pith helmets and native porters are long gone. Missionary work today is incredibly varied. Missionaries can still be found working in remote parts of the African bush, but they can also be found serving their Lord in some of the major cities of the world, with all the problems of urban decay and deprivation. Indeed, many of these cities are not just third-world cities. Whereas at one stage Africa, Asia, and South America together with the Caribbean formed the focus of missionary concern, now Europe is very much a mission field too. For instance at the time of writing the Baptist Missionary Society works not only in Angola, Brazil, El Salvador, India, Jamaica, Nepal, Nicaragua, Sri Lanka, Thailand, Trinidad, and Zaire, but also in Belgium and France, and has been invited to work in such countries as Italy and Albania.

Another change is the length of service given by missionaries: those who spend the whole of their working life overseas are increasingly rare; whereas an increasing number of young people are going abroad for just a few months with BMS 28:19 teams.

Even more fundamental has been the way in which relationships have been transformed with partner churches overseas – indeed, the very term 'partner church' is itself a recognition that the old days of paternalism are well and truly over. None of these developments are peculiar to the BMS. However, it is fair to say that the BMS has been at the forefront in the development of new patterns of mission. Yet for all the developments and changes, at its heart the task is still the same as in Carey's day: the implementation of Matthew 28:19.

Although the BMS was obviously the first Baptist missionary society, it is now but a senior partner amongst many others. While the BMS acts as the overseas missionary agency for the Baptist churches in the UK, many other Baptist Unions and Conventions have their own missionary societies: e.g. the Australian Baptist Missionary Society, the New Zealand Baptist Missionary Society, the Board of International Missionaries of the American Baptist Churches, the Foreign Mission Board of the Southern Baptist Convention. In Continental Europe a number of Baptist Unions have come together to form the European Baptist Mission.

TO THINK ABOUT . . .

It used to be said: 'It is in the missionary meeting that you hear the beating of the Baptist heart.'

Is that true today? If not, why not?

SUMMARY

Although mission is certainly not restricted to Baptists, Baptists are unashamedly a missionary people. They have always been passionately concerned to share their faith and to demonstrate God's love for all. It is no exaggeration to say that the Great Commission is engraved on Baptist hearts. As radical believers they take seriously the charge of the risen Lord.

Conclusion

– a heritage to own –

The title of this book and the thesis of its chapters is that the Baptist way of being the church produces radical believers. As a direct result of seeking to root their life together in the Scriptures, Baptist churches inevitably have a radical edge in comparison with the more established churches.

On the other hand, honesty compels us to admit that the reality of present-day Baptist church life does not always correspond with the radicalism of those convictions traditionally held by Baptists. In spite of their dissenting tradition, Baptists can be as conformist as any other Christian church or denomination.

Hopefully, however, this presentation of those principles undergirding the Baptist way of being the church will cause Baptists to re-think the way they express their life together. How true are we to our heritage? How true are we to those Scriptures upon which our heritage is based? The Reformation cry – 'reformed and being reformed' – needs to be on Baptist lips too. There is never a time when we can afford to sit back on our laurels, thinking we have 'made it' as a church. A sense of holy discontent should be the hallmark of every Baptist church, as it constantly seeks to be true to its calling. For no church can stand still – ongoing renewal is here to stay.

We therefore wish to challenge churches and their leaders to take a fresh look at the way in which they live their life together. Maybe what is called for is not so much a mission-audit, but rather a heritage-audit.

Yet this book has not been written just to challenge the churches to review their life together. Another intention has been to spell out that very distinct identity which is peculiar to Baptists. True, Baptists have much in common with other Christians. True, all the various Baptist emphases are held by one or other Christian church. But nowhere else are all these emphases found held together, save in Baptist churches. What is more, all these emphases are rooted in Scripture, and as such they are worth standing for. Baptists can – and should – be rightly proud of their heritage, because it is a heritage which has always sought to express God's way of being the church. True Baptists, therefore, are not simply Baptists by convenience or by accident, but rather by conviction. Let this book be a challenge to all Baptists to own their heritage.

> *TO THINK ABOUT . . .*
> **Return to page 9 and to the first question.**
> **How will your answer to that question be**
> **different in the future?**

APPENDIX A

An Historical Perspective

ROOTS

With a world-wide membership of some thirty-seven million baptised believers, Baptists form one of the major streams within the Christian Church. Baptist strength, however, is not equally spread geographically. In North America they are a force to be reckoned with, whilst in other parts of the world Baptists are sometimes a tiny minority, scorned as a 'sect', even by other churches which should know better.

Baptists are not only large in numbers but also orthodox in belief and happily affirm the tenets of all the major creeds of the church. Yet, while orthodox in belief, Baptists have been marked by a radicalism in practice. They have tried to find their roots in Scripture rather than the traditions that have been added through many centuries.

Baptists have never set out to form a separate denomination. First and foremost they have sought to mirror the life and faith of the New Testament church. Although Baptists have never claimed to be the one and only expression of the church of God, there is no doubt that Baptists, through their enthusiastic commitment to the faith of the New Testament church, have kept the flag of the gospel flying at times when the spiritual life of the state churches has been at a very low ebb. It is therefore no exaggeration to say that the whole Christian church has much cause to be grateful to Baptists for their radical witness.

When did Baptists begin? Baptists like to find their ultimate roots in Scripture, but from a strictly historical perspective they are children of the Reformation. Their precise parentage, however, is open to dispute. Some trace their beginnings back to the Anabaptists of sixteenth-century continental Europe, others to the Puritans and Separatists of seventeenth-century England. Probably the most helpful way of approaching Baptist beginnings is to view Baptist life as a river into which flow a number of streams. Which precisely may be termed the river's source is an academic issue of little practical consequence as the various streams merge into the one strong waterway.

THOSE DANGEROUS REVOLUTIONARIES

EUROPEAN ANABAPTISTS

In popular mythology the Continental Reformation is often depicted as a power struggle between the Roman Catholics on the one hand and the great Reformers on the other. In fact the situation was much more complex. For alongside the Roman Catholics and the emerging Protestant state churches of Martin Luther, John Calvin, and Ulrich Zwingli, were also the 'Anabaptists', the radicals of the Reformation.

From an Anabaptist perspective the Reformers did not go far enough. In particular, for all their emphasis on justification by faith, they failed to take this emphasis to its logical conclusion in a believers' church. The result was that they too were locked into the concept of a state church to which all belonged, with or without faith. It was the Anabaptist understanding of the *church* – not just of baptism – which was their distinctive legacy.

The prefix 'ana' is Greek in origin and, like the Latin prefix 're', simply means 'again': the 'Anabaptists' were the 'Rebaptisers'. They rejected the concept of infant baptism and practised the baptism of believers, which in sixteenth-century Europe, where infant baptism was well-nigh universal, inevitably involved re-baptising – or so it seemed to those practising infant baptism.

The stance on believers' baptism was, therefore, perceived as a real threat to the establishment of the day. In stressing the need for individuals to find faith in Christ prior to baptism, the Anabaptists were to all intents and purposes undermining the unity of church and state, which had existed since the conversion of Constantine, the first Roman emperor to become a Christian.

Up until Constantine's conversion in AD 312 the Christian church was a persecuted minority and was essentially a believers' church. Once the Christian faith became the official religion of the empire, many people became members of the church not out of religious conviction, but rather out of expediency. Whereas in the past membership of the Christian church might have been a bar to advancement, now it became advantageous, if not necessary, for official favour and promotion. From the point of view of later church history, Constantine's conversion may have been a disaster!

In sixteenth-century Europe, as a result of the developed 'Constantinian' pattern of the unity of church and state, to be a member of the state – a citizen – automatically involved being a member of the state church. Refusing your children baptism into the state church was perceived, therefore, as an act of political defiance, not just an act of ecclesiastical dissent. So the Anabaptists were ruthlessly persecuted by Protestants and Roman Catholics alike. They were regarded as dangerous revolutionaries and many thousands were burned at the stake or drowned in rivers and lakes.

Some Anabaptists certainly did go to extremes in thought and behaviour, feeding the propaganda against them all, but the vast majority were godly people concerned above all to follow Jesus Christ. Taking seriously the teaching of Jesus in the Sermon on the Mount, they rejected the swearing of oaths and the concept of a 'just' war. They were radical Christians in the sense that they allowed Scripture to be their guide. When, for instance, their opponents claimed that they had Zwingli's word on a situation, the Ana-

baptists replied that they had God's Word on it! They were revolutionary not so much in the way they separated church from state, but rather in the way they allowed the gospel to impinge upon every aspect of life.

Whether or not there is a direct link between Anabaptists and Baptists as we know them today is a matter of dispute. However, the spirit of the Anabaptists certainly characterised the life of many of our Baptist forefathers, and the more recent availability of Anabaptist writings in English has again influenced a number of Baptist thinkers.

ENGLISH NONCONFORMISTS

The English Nonconformists emerged from the sixteenth-century Puritan movement. The Puritans felt that the English Reformation had not been thorough enough. At first they campaigned from within the Church of England for further changes. In time many became impatient and, in the words of Robert Browne's famous tract, set on foot a reformation 'without tarrying for any', and separated from the national church.

Many Puritans became persuaded that the only right way to understand the church was as a voluntary, gathered and covenanted community of believers. These 'Separatists' formed congregations of believers – which were the first Independent or Congregational churches. In time some of them saw believers' baptism as biblical and so the first Baptist churches were formed.

Along with the Congregationalists and Presbyterians, English Baptists were known as 'Nonconformists'. In the first place Baptists were non-conformist in refusing to conform to and be members of the Church of England. If Christ was to be king of the church, then the church had to be free of state control.

The call to nonconformity is not only to resist the identification of church and state, but also to resist the world. In the words of the apostle Paul, we are called not to be 'conformed to this world', but rather to be 'transformed' by the renewing of our minds (Romans 12:2). The first English Baptists with their Puritan streak were true to this further emphasis. They were 'dissenters' in every sense of the word.

BIBLE-BELIEVING CHRISTIANS

In 1602 a group of English Separatists under the leadership of John Smyth (?1570–1612), who had been an Anglican clergyman, formed a church at Gainsborough and

> as the Lord's free people, joined themselves (by a covenant of the Lord) into a church determined in the fellowship of the Gospel, to walk in all his ways, made known or to be made known unto them (according to their best endeavours), whatsoever it should cost them, the Lord assisting them.

Because of persecution, the Gainsborough group fled to Holland, settling in the Amsterdam bakehouse of Jan Munter, a leading Mennonite. John Smyth's fellow leader was Thomas Helwys, a lawyer from Nottingham.

Smyth spent his time in Amsterdam wrestling with the Scriptures as he sought to discover the true nature of the church. 'As a result of study of the Word', in 1609 Smyth came to see believers' baptism as the New Testament norm for entry into the church. He thereupon baptised first himself, and then Helwys and the rest of the group. They baptised by affusion, pouring or sprinkling water over the candidate, but within a few years baptism by immersion was established as Baptist practice.

For Smyth, as for other Separatists, the Scriptures were the deciding factor for all matters of faith and practice. They were Bible-believing Christians, resolved to pattern their life and faith upon the Scriptures. They had a dynamic understanding of the Scriptures, and were committed to an ongoing exploration of the Word of God. As John Robinson, another English Separatist leader in Holland, put it 'The Lord hath yet more light and truth to break forth from his Word'.

This emphasis upon the authority of Scripture is part of our Baptist heritage. We have always understood Scripture as the controlling factor in establishing doctrine. In 1644, for instance, another Baptist group declared:

> The Rule of this Knowledge, Faith, and Obedience, concerning the worship and service of God, and all other Christian duties, is not mans inventions, opinions, devices, lawes, constitutions, or traditions unwritten whatsoever, but only the word of God contained in the Canonical Scriptures.
>
> 1644 *Particular Baptist Confession*, section vii

Baptists are not alone in their high view of Scripture, but they have made a particular point of being 'people of the book'.

Whereas some of the great state churches have sought to maintain a balance between 'scripture', 'tradition' and 'reason', Baptists have declared emphatically that Scripture, and Scripture alone, must have the last word. Hence the desire of Baptists to model the life of their churches on that of the New Testament church. In a very real sense, Baptists are 'restorationists': they have sought to restore the church in the light of principles discovered in Scripture.

Baptists generally have been fairly conservative in their approach to the Scriptures, although sadly they have not always been agreed about what this entails. At the time of the Evangelical Revival, eighteenth-century Baptists were slow to grasp the new outlook, although effective once they eventually embraced the Great Commission. In the nineteenth century they were so protective of the Scriptures that they were slow to accept the benefits from new biblical scholarship. In recent years the Southern Baptist Convention of the United States has been bitterly divided over the precise nature of Biblical revelation, polarising Christians who all respect the authority of Scripture. Most Baptists believe that the Bible is the infallible Word of God, at least in the sense that it is entirely trustworthy for the purposes for which God inspired its writers, to guide people to salvation and to a better way of life. Because it is trustworthy, it is therefore authoritative.

One temptation for Christians is to imprison God's Word in cages of orthodoxy, rather than letting it disturb their comfortable lives. A 'conservative' approach to Scripture – as in the term 'conservative evangelical' – should inevitably lead to a 'radical' outlook on life. Strictly speaking, we should be 'radical evangelicals'. We need to get back to our revolutionary roots!

FREEDOM-FIGHTERS

In 1612 Thomas Helwys, while still in Amsterdam, wrote *A Short Declaration of the Mistery of Iniquity*, which is generally considered the first claim for freedom of religion published in English and he sent a copy to King James I. In magisterial style Helwys declared:

> for men's religion to God, is betwixt God and themselves; the King shall not answer for it, neither may the King be judge between God and man. Let them be heretics, Turks [i.e. Muslims], Jews, or whatsoever it appertains not to the earthly power to punish them in the least measure. This is made evident to our lord the King by the scriptures.

Note that Helwys was arguing not just for Baptists to be free to worship God as they liked, but for adherents of *any* religion to be free to worship God in whatever way they deemed right. Helwys was a man born before his time. Not surprisingly on his return to England, he was put in prison by James I, where he remained until he died.

Baptists have long prided themselves on their stand for religious freedom. Roger Williams, for instance, who in 1631 emigrated from England to America to escape the persecution of Archbishop Laud, was a passionate advocate of religious freedom. Banished from Massachusetts in 1638 because of his views on the separation of church and state, Williams founded the Rhode Island Colony in 1638, where religious freedom became a key policy. In 1639 he became a Baptist, and in 1644 published a famous defence of liberty of conscience entitled *The Bloudy Tenant of Persecution for Cause Conscience*.

Throughout the Stuart period Baptists and their fellow dissenters suffered persecution. Laws prohibited their meetings, and, when they persisted, their goods were confiscated and their preachers were imprisoned. Many emigrated to America in search of greater freedom, and there was regular contact between Baptists on both sides of the Atlantic; later Baptist sympathies were to lie with the colonists rather than King George during the American War of Independence. At home Baptist support for Cromwell was hardly surprising and they enjoyed a respite during the Commonwealth period; many new churches were founded in those years. With the Restoration of Charles II, persecution was renewed. The Act of Toleration of 1689, following the accession of William and Mary, made life easier and dissenters were allowed to worship in peace, but they were still denied full civil rights. These were only won bit by bit through the nineteenth century. For much of their history, English Baptists have been involved in the struggle for freedom to worship God in their own chosen way without incurring civil penalties.

A former English Baptist leader, H. Wheeler Robinson, declared: 'The Baptist tabernacle is not always a graceful structure, but at least we may say this of it, that the twin pillars at its door are evangelism and liberty'. In the dining hall of Regent's Park College, the Baptist theological college in Oxford, a five-pointed star sums up Baptist emphases: 'Faith, Baptism, Evangelism, Fellowship, and Freedom'.

To what extent are Baptists free to believe and advocate what they will? Are there parameters of religious belief within which Baptists are constrained to abide if they are to remain Baptists? Traditionally Baptists have distanced themselves from creeds as tests of religious faith, although in the past they often produced confessions of faith which sought positively to affirm those things they held in common.

This emphasis on freedom has led Baptists to espouse the general cause of human rights. In Jamaica, for instance, under the leadership of William Knibb, Baptists were instrumental in bringing about the end of the slave trade in 1834. More recently Baptists have made a costly stand for human rights in such countries as Angola and El Salvador. Whether Baptists today in general can be characterised by a passion for religious freedom is perhaps open to question. The torch at times seems to have been passed on to others.

GENERAL AND PARTICULAR BAPTISTS

TWO STREAMS EMERGE

For much of their history Baptists have wrestled with the doctrine of the Cross of Christ, particularly as it relates to the sovereignty and grace of God. Indeed, as far as England is concerned, there have been two streams of Baptists: General Baptists and Particular Baptists. The General Baptists were influenced by the teaching of the Dutch theologian, Arminius, and believed in 'general' redemption: i.e. when Christ died on the Cross, he died for all. Particular Baptists, however, were influenced by the writings of John Calvin, and believed in 'particular' redemption: i.e. when Christ died on the Cross, he died for a 'particular' group of men and women – the 'elect'.

The Baptists in Amsterdam were Arminian in their theology, and were, therefore, the first General Baptists. Soon after a stream of Particular Baptists emerged. This latter group had its origins in an Independent (Congregational) Calvinistic church formed in 1616, which around 1633 formed a new fellowship under the leadership of Samuel Eaton, who began to practise believers' baptism. By 1644 these Particular Baptists had established a number of churches, and they produced a *Confession of Faith*, which not only affirmed their belief that believers' baptism by immersion was the New Testament norm, but also upheld the classic five 'tulip' points of Calvinism:

- **T**otal Depravity (there is no aspect of our nature which is left intact by sin);
- **U**nconditional Election (God chooses whom he wills);
- **L**imited Atonement (Christ died only for the elect);
- **I**rresistible Grace (God saves those whom he wills to save);
- [Final] **P**erseverance of the Saints (once saved, always saved).

Most Baptists today are ignorant of the five points of Calvinism and have little interest in debating the pros and cons of 'particular' as opposed to 'general' redemption, but these were important issues for our forefathers. Some may find it illuminating to look further at these matters (see the books suggested at the end of this appendix). Some of the old insights, like Calvin's high view of the church, may be rediscovered to advantage.

THE MISSIONARY MOVEMENT EMERGES

The Particular Baptists proved to be the backbone of English Baptists. During the eighteenth century the General Baptists declined in number and many became Unitarian in theology, but the Particular Baptists held their own and remained orthodox in theology.

Admittedly many Particular Baptists became exceedingly inward-looking until, under the influence of the American Congregationalist, Jonathan Edwards, they developed a real concern to share the gospel with others and grew in consequence. Jonathan Edwards, although a Calvinist, contended that 'it is God's manner to make use of means in carrying on his work in the world'. This evangelical Calvinism was made accessible to English Baptists by their theologian, Andrew Fuller. William Carey, the great missionary pioneer took up this theme of 'means' when in 1792 he published *An Enquiry into the Obligation of Christians to use means for the Conversion of the Heathens*. The Baptist Missionary Society, founded by Carey and his friends in 1792, was first known as 'The Particular Baptist Society for Propagating the Gospel among the Heathen'.

C.H. Spurgeon, the nineteenth-century Baptist 'prince of preachers', also combined a Calvinistic theology with a passion for evangelism. He once picturesquely spoke of a Christian entering heaven through an arch. As he entered he saw written over the arch the words, 'Whosoever believes shall not perish, but have everlasting life', but as he looked back he saw written over the arch the words 'You have not chosen me, but I have chosen you'.

THE NEW CONNEXION

Whilst the majority of the General or Arminian Baptists were drawn towards Unitarianism, some remained orthodox Trinitarians. Under the influence of John Wesley and the evangelical revival, a new Connexion of General Baptists was formed in 1770. Central to the leadership of this new grouping was Dan Taylor (1738–1816). He was a Yorkshire miner and, although converted among the Methodists, came to Baptist convictions by his own study of the New Testament. Taylor was introduced to the General Baptists of the Midlands and met Samuel Deacon, another important figure in the formation and leadership of the New Connexion of General Baptists.

Taylor was a vigorous leader, and many new churches were formed in the heartland of the New Connexion in the new industrial towns of the Midlands and the North. In 1790 Taylor wrote an *Essay on the Truth and Inspiration of Holy Scripture* and in 1798 he founded an academy for the training of New Connexion ministers. In 1816 the New Connexion formed its own Missionary Society.

Following increasingly closer links with the Particular Baptists, the New Connexion became integrated into the Baptist Union in 1891.

[Not all Baptist churches in England became members of the Baptist Union of Great Britain. Some have remained independent congregations. A relatively small group of churches, known as Strict and Particular Baptists, formed their own associations. These churches clung to a strict Calvinistic theology, and firmly kept their communion tables closed to all but baptised believers. Many of these Strict and Particular Baptist churches are now known as 'Grace' Baptist churches.]

A DEVELOPING STORY

THE NINETEENTH CENTURY

The nineteenth century was an era of particularly strong growth amongst Baptists. They were gradually winning full civil rights and throwing off the old image of dissent. The many imposing new chapels, designed to accommodate the huge congregations coming to hear the Victorian pulpit orators, were a far cry from the simple meeting houses of earlier generations. Increasingly aware of the problems of the industrial society at home and of troubles abroad, especially the evils of slavery and concerns about free trade, Baptists found they often needed to work in units larger than the local church. They joined with other Baptists in support of missionary bodies at home as well as overseas, and joined with other evangelical Christians in developing education for the people and in fighting abuses. The old love of freedom now took on the language of voluntaryism: they would willingly work with others in voluntary institutions, but continued to resist any suggestion of coercion.

In spite of their good working relationships with evangelical Anglicans, Baptists vigorously campaigned for the disestablishment of the Church of England. They were also very disturbed by the activities of Tractarians and Ritualists, who were renewing aspects of Anglican life but in ways that seemed to Baptists too much like Roman Catholicism. In reaction, Baptists became even more wary in their own church life of anything 'sacramental' or mysterious.

These were the days of great pulpit giants, whom people thronged to hear. Robert Hall was pre-eminent at the start of the century, to be followed later by men like Alexander McLaren, the great Bible expositor who ministered in Manchester from 1858 to 1903, John Clifford, the General Baptist minister at Westbourne Park, Paddington, and Charles Haddon Spurgeon. Spurgeon and Clifford, along with many others, had a passion to meet both the spiritual and social needs of their day. In spite of the turbulence of doctrinal debate – marked by Spurgeon's withdrawal from the Baptist Union in 1888 – they were halcyon days for Baptists.

THE TWENTIETH CENTURY

English Baptist life in the twentieth century has been less impressive. Like other mainline churches in Britain, Baptists went into severe numerical decline. Historians and sociologists debate the causes: was the shock of the First World War to blame, or was the rise of theological liberalism the culprit? Or was it a combination of both, in that the First World War exposed the shallowness of theological liberalism?

In the 1970s the tide of defeatism and decline began to turn and in the 1980s a new spirit of optimism and commitment to church growth and church planting emerged. What is the explanation for this turn-around? The hand of God apart – and ultimately he gives the growth (1 Cor 3:6–7) – from a human perspective we can identify at least four factors responsible for recent renewed Baptist confidence.

A growing evangelical identity

In one sense Baptists have always been evangelical – the practice of believers' baptism inevitably emphasises the need for repentance and faith. So Baptists have been among the chief beneficiaries of the general evangelical renaissance in England during the past twenty to thirty years.

An openness to charismatic renewal

Charismatic renewal, which first came to Britain in the 1960s, has influenced far more Baptist churches than the twenty per cent which in a recent survey (1989) identified themselves as charismatic. In spite of inevitable excesses, the threefold emphasis on the worship of God, on 'body life' (note the growth of small groups), and spiritual gifts, has revitalised many Baptists.

The influence of church-growth thinking

Baptists played a key role in the 1980s when the insights of the American church-growth school were introduced to Britain. In what had been basically a survival situation, the church-growth movement, with its clear-cut conviction that God intends his church to grow, proved revolutionary for many Baptists.

The ongoing commitment to evangelism and social action

Baptists have always been a missionary people. Where a church is committed evangelically, influenced charismatically, and convinced that Jesus is building his church, there evangelism is likely to become increasingly effective.

All four of these factors were present in the formation of Mainstream, a Baptist 'ginger' group promoting 'life and growth' within the churches and structures of the denomination. Evidence of this new life and growth came unexpectedly in 1979 when a working group, set up in 1977 to examine 'the causes for the numerical and spiritual decline' of the Baptist Union, produced a report entitled *Signs of Hope*. The report concluded that:

> there does seem to be a new move towards more openness and less hypocrisy, a greater sense of flexibility and an unwillingness to be bound by precedent, a new concern to proclaim the eternal gospel in terms relevant to the contemporary scene, and a greater willingness to serve the needs of the community in the name of Christ.

In the twentieth century some Baptists have become involved in the Liturgical Movement, and their influence has been felt widely in the churches. Stephen Winward, for example, challenged the way the communion service had become almost an afterthought tacked on after the 'main' service. Now many churches incorporate celebration of the Lord's Supper more centrally in worship.

In recent years, too, there has been a renewed understanding that evangelism is closely allied to social concern and action. A tendency had developed earlier in the twentieth century for churches to focus especially on one or the other, making their witness less fully true to the gospel and prompting divisive attitudes. The fresh emphasis on 'holistic mission' is a further sign of life and new hope among Baptists today.

Currently there are some 2150 churches with a total membership of almost 160,000, in the Baptist Union of Great Britain (a union largely English, but with a significant Welsh and tiny Scottish representation).

BAPTISTS BEYOND ENGLAND

OTHER PARTS OF THE UK

Baptists in the other parts of the United Kingdom also have a long history. The first Baptist church in Wales was established in 1650, in Scotland by 1652, in Ireland in the early 1650s. Their fortunes too have been mixed: the Welsh, for instance, benefited significantly from the Welsh Revival of 1904, but have since suffered great decline. In 1990 the Baptist Union of Wales had 27,700 members in 560 churches.

The Baptist Union of Scotland, although relatively small, has for many years been marked by evangelistic fervour. In 1991 they numbered 15,166 members in 166 churches. The Baptist Union of Ireland covers the whole island and is more conservative than other Baptist groups in the United Kingdom. It is, however, a growing Union and in 1990 had 101 churches with 8550 members.

BAPTISTS WORLD-WIDE

Baptists are not confined to the United Kingdom, but are found throughout the world. The Baptist World Alliance reports almost thirty-seven million baptised members of Baptist churches, representing a community of at least seventy million people. This forms probably the largest Protestant denomination in the world today. Although Baptists are strongest in North America, where various Baptist groupings claim over thirty million members, Baptist numbers are significant in many other parts of the world: for example, Baptists have experienced strong growth recently in Brazil and Korea.

EUROPE

The one continent where Baptists are struggling is Europe. With less than 700,000 members overall, European Baptists are either in decline or just holding their own. Although Baptists are found in almost every country in Europe, they only have real numerical strength in Germany, Sweden, the Commonwealth of Independent States and the United Kingdom.

The most significant Baptist figure in Continental European history was the German, Johann Gerhard Oncken (1800–1884), 'The Father of Continental Baptists'. Converted on a visit to Scotland, he and six others were eventually baptised in 1834 in the River Elbe and formed the first German Baptist Church. Under Oncken's strong leadership the Baptist cause began to spread southwards and eastwards, and churches were quickly planted both in Germany and beyond, for example in Denmark, Lithuania, and Switzerland.

It has been said that the main impetus for Baptist growth in continental Europe came from three principal sources:

- the missionary zeal of German Baptists under Oncken's leadership;
- missionary support from British and American Baptists;
- the earnest desire on the part of converts to share their new-found faith after Baptist churches had been organized in their respective countries.

With new opportunities in Europe, both East and West, and with English increasingly becoming Europe's first language there are new opportunities for British Baptists in missionary involvement in Europe.

The story of the English Baptists has been told more fully by Roger Hayden in a companion volume to this, entitled *English Baptist History and Heritage* (published by the Baptist Union of Great Britain); by Barrie White in *The English Baptists of the 17th Century* and Raymond Brown in *The English Baptists of the 18th Century* published by The Baptist Historical Society).

APPENDIX B

The following statement was approved by the European Baptist Federation Council, meeting at Hoddesdon, England, in September 1992.

What are Baptists?

– a Statement of Identity by Baptist Christians in Europe –

INTRODUCTION

1. The following document is *not intended as a confession of faith*, but an explanation as to who Baptists are; inevitably, however, it includes certain affirmations about faith and gospel. The statement is not meant to compel assent or to replace the confessions of faith of the different Baptist Unions. It is offered as just *one* tool for communication in explaining Baptists to the representatives of other Christian churches. In addition to separate pieces of literature about Baptist identity produced by the various Unions, it seemed good to try and produce one piece by the EBF acting together. When finally issued in leaflet form, it will be accompanied by a longer piece about the *history* of Baptist churches in Europe than is possible within the compass of this statement.

2. In the light of some reactions it must be underlined that the document is descriptive, recording both agreements and differences in practice between Baptists. There is no attempt being made to alter the convictions of certain Baptist Unions, or to produce any uniformity.

3. The 13 clauses were originally put together as the summary of the work of discussion groups at the Consultation on Baptist Mission in Dorfweil, Germany (26–29 January 1992). In the plenary session the 13 clauses were approved in principle, though the wording was recognised to be provisional. The *Division of Theology and Education*, through its Convenor, was given the responsibility of preparing a draft document, including the adding of paragraphs of extra explanation to each clause; those present at the Consultation asked that these paragraphs should reflect the *range of opinion* which had been expressed in their various discussion groups. The document was then sent to Baptist Unions throughout Europe for comment. Their responses were carefully considered, and were reported to the meeting of the European Baptist Teachers of Theology in July 1992 when the document was discussed and refined. However, the teachers made no attempt to produce an agreed statement. To aid further revision, three consultants were appointed from the Teachers' Conference, representing Eastern and Western Europe.

STATEMENT

1. *We are part of the whole, world-wide Christian Church and we confess faith in One God as Father, Son and Holy Spirit.*

Baptists understand themselves to be part of a continuing stream of Christian truth and devotion that has flowed from New Testament times. However, they trace the more immediate origin of their congregations to the period of the Protestant Reformation in Europe, and are indebted to the recovery at that time of the biblical principle of 'justification by God's grace through faith alone'.

While Baptists have traditionally refused to bind themselves to creeds, following the Reformation watchword of 'Scripture alone', they have always recognised such early statements as the Creed of

Nicaea, the Definition of Chalcedon and 'The Apostles' Creed' as being true witnesses to the Christian faith. Holding faith in the triune God, Baptists share basic beliefs with other Christian churches, including: God's work as Creator; the fallen nature of human beings; the perfect humanity and deity of Jesus Christ, who is God manifest in a human person; redemption through the life, atoning death and resurrection of Christ; the transforming of personal and social life by the power of the Holy Spirit; and the final fulfilment of God's purposes.

The first Baptist church, in the modern sense, gathered in London in 1611. Its immediate roots lay in small groups of believers within England which had separated from the State Church during the period of the English Reformation in the 16th century, but it was also shaped by Reformation movements on the continent of Europe. Several of its founding members had lived for a while in Holland where they had sought religious liberty, and where they had been influenced by successors of the earlier continental 'Anabaptist' movement which had begun in Zürich, with its emphasis upon Christian discipleship and baptism of believers.

Baptist churches on the continent of Europe outside Great Britain were mainly established in the 19th century, drawing upon new movements of Christian pietism with Germany and Scandanavia at that time, and with some help from Baptist churches in Britain and North America. Baptists in Central and Eastern Europe feel a specially close connection with the Anabaptists who had an impact upon the society of their countries in earlier times, although their link with them is more of a spiritual kinship than a clear historical continuity. Today there are Baptist Unions in nearly every European country, linked in fellowship through the European Baptist Federation. The Baptist World Alliance, formed in 1905, joins together some 38 million Baptists in over 150 countries throughout the world.

2. *We affirm the need for personal faith in Jesus Christ and for discipleship in his likeness.*

Baptists believe that every Christian person should be able to attest his or her own trust in Jesus Christ as Saviour and Lord; the personal story of faith will include repentance towards God the Father and renewal of life by the Holy Spirit of God. Such an experience of the grace of God should lead to a radical discipleship which reflects the manner of life of Jesus Christ, and which should shape ethics and action not only in the church but in wider society.

3. *Our final authority in faith and practice is Jesus Christ, as revealed in the Scriptures and present among his people through the Holy Spirit.*

Baptists recognise the rule of Jesus Christ, the Son of God risen from the dead, and present today to guide believers into all truth whenever they gather together in his name. His rule takes precedence over all other authorities. In order to discern and interpret the authority of Christ among them, Baptists appeal in the first place to the Scriptures, believing these to be the means by which all sources of truth about God are to be assessed and judged.

4. *We recognise the Scriptures of the Old and New Testaments as the primary authority for knowing God's revelation in Christ.*

Baptists believe that God speaks his word to human beings through the Scriptures, which are inspired by his Spirit. They usually think it right to call the Scriptures 'the word of God', because the written word witnesses to God's supreme Word which is Jesus Christ. All teaching of Christian doctrine, including creeds and tradition, must therefore be tested by its harmony with Scripture. Baptists expect the church to be continually reformed by hearing the word of God through Scripture, and they also expect new light to spring forth from Scripture by the power of the Holy Spirit in every generation. While individual believers must always allow their interpretation of Scripture to be illuminated by the understanding of the wider Christian community, they have the final right to judge for themselves what God is saying to them through the word and by the Spirit.

5. *We understand the Church to be a fellowship of believers, sharing the table of the Lord.*

Baptists understand the church to be made up of believers who have covenanted with each other and with God to worship and work together. They have often spoken of themselves as being a 'gathered community', meaning *both* that God has called them together as the Body of Christ visible in one place, *and* that they have voluntarily agreed so to meet. Their mutual life is expressed in gathering around the table where the Lord's Supper is celebrated in bread and wine, and they believe that here they are also in fellowship with the whole Body of Jesus Christ which is the world-wide Church.

6. *We practise baptism, for believers only, into the Body of Christ.*

Baptists find that baptism in the New Testament and the earliest church was normally immersion into water, in the triune name of God, of those who could confess their personal allegiance to Jesus Christ as Lord. A person must therefore have faith before being baptised; in baptism there is a coming together of this human faith with the grace of God as the believer shares in the death and resurrection of Christ, so also bearing witness to salvation. All this makes the act inappropriate for infants.

Baptism is inseparable from entrance into membership of the church as the Body of Christ, though Baptists allow freedom of conscience among themselves about the way this is to be worked out. Many churches insist that those joining the church must first be baptised as believers; others, recognising with sadness the broken nature of the Church Universal, will accept those who have been baptised as infants and confirmed in other Christian churches; still others, in special circumstances, will permit membership simply on confession of personal faith in Christ.

Notwithstanding such differences, all Baptists believe that a return to the New Testament practice of believers' baptism is essential for true understanding of the nature of faith, the church and discipleship.

7. *We affirm the freedom and the responsibility of each local congregation to discover the purpose of Christ for its own life and work.*

Members of local Baptist churches gather in a 'Church Meeting' to arrange their own affairs, both practical and spiritual, under the rule of Christ. Decisions concerning every area of church life, including the ordering of worship and the calling of a minister to serve among them, are taken by consent of the meeting. Important decisions are usually reached through a democratic process of voting, but the aim of the meeting is not for groups to win votes for their cause, but for everyone to find the purpose of Christ for his church. Although the local church is legally independent, it will recognise its spiritual inter-dependence with others in its aim to find the mind of Christ, and will for example be open to the views of other churches with which it is in fellowship.

8. *We affirm the 'priesthood of all believers', in which all members of the church are called to ministry; but some are called to exercise spiritual leadership, which is always to be understood as serving.*

Baptists hold that all believers are called to serve Christ in his church and in the world, and that for this task the Holy Spirit distributes gifts to the whole people of God. They expect to find a whole range of spiritual gifts in a local church, with members exercising variously such gifts as teaching, evangelism, pastoring, guiding, serving, prophetic insight, knowledge, praying, healing, administration and hospitality. These ministries are both for the building up of the church and for the bringing of healing and reconciliation into every area of daily life and work.

Baptists also believe, however, that Christ calls some to exercise a ministry of spiritual leadership, with particular responsibilities for preaching, teaching and pastoral care. Among Baptists there has generally been a two-fold office of 'minister' and 'deacons'. A local church appoints a group of deacons from among its own members to serve with the minister, although some churches also now appoint a number of 'elders' who generally have greater pastoral responsibility. Church members gathered in the church meeting are responsible for testing and recognising whether people have in fact received these various calls from God to serve among them.

Within this accepted pattern, Baptist churches show some differences in their understanding of spiritual leadership. Most ordain their ministers by laying on of hands, after they have completed their theological education. Some recognise the call of both men and women to be ministers, while others recognise only men. Each Baptist church has the freedom to invite someone to serve it as minister, but some Baptist Unions will only designate as 'ministers' those who have had their vocation tested and approved by a wider group of churches than a single local church, thus recognising them as ministers of the Church Universal. All Baptists, however, recognise that the local church acting on its own authority can appoint some of its members as 'deacons' or 'elders'. Within some Unions of churches, senior ministers are appointed to have pastoral care over a whole assocation of churches, though their authority lies in the giving of counsel to a local church and its minister rather than exercising executive power over them.

Despite differences, Baptists believe that it is the coming together of believers into fellowship that calls for spiritual oversight, rather than thinking that the existence of a spiritual leader creates a church.

9. We believe that the mutual commitment expressed in baptism and in membership of the local church should lead to wider partnerships between churches wherever possible.

From the beginning of their history, local Baptist churches have sought fellowship with other churches, for mutual encouragement, guidance, sharing of mission and as a sign of reconciliation for the world. Baptist churches form local associations with other Baptist churches, coming together into a Union of churches at national level. Many (though not all) Unions and their member churches also share in ecumenical partnerships in both national and international councils.

10. We believe that every Christian disciple is called to witness to the Lordship of Jesus Christ, and that the Church as a part of God's Kingdom is to share in the whole mission of God in the world.

Baptists believe that each Christian disciple is called to speak of his or her own personal faith to others, and to take an active part in the spreading of the gospel of Christ throughout the world. Since mission includes both evangelism and social concern, Baptists also believe that they are to give expression to God's love for humankind through meeting people's physical as well as spiritual needs. The coming of God's sovereign rule is, however, wider than the Church and Baptists recognise God's call to share with him in his work of creating justice, social welfare, healing, education and peace in the world.

11. We affirm the need to preserve freedom of conscience, and so we accept differences among us.

Baptists have throughout their history urged governments to pass laws enshrining freedom of conscience, including freedom in matters of religious belief and worship. At the same time Baptists encourage a spiritual freedom among their churches; wlthin a common commitment to Jesus Christ and a broad Baptist identity, they welcome and accept differences of outlook and diversity of practice.

12. We stand for the separation of church and state, rooted in the sole lordship of Christ and concern for religious liberty.

Baptists have always pressed for the separation of the *institutions* of the church and the state, meaning that the state should have no power to legislate over matters of religious belief or have any part in the government of the church. Correspondingly, the church must oppose the state's passing of laws which would give more privileges to religious believers, or to a certain denomination of them, than to other citizens. It also means that no country or section of it can be designated by the state as the preserve of a particular part of the Christian Church or of any non-Christian religion.

On the other hand, Baptists show a sense of responsibility for the state, and most churches encourage their members to become actively involved in politics and to take posts within the civil authorities. They also believe that the Church as a whole must speak with a prophetic voice in criticism of the state where it falls short of God's intention for it, and in favour of its activities when these accord with God's purposes.

13. *As Christian believers, we live in hope of the final appearing of Christ in glory, and the transforming of all creation.*

Having hope in God's future, when the lordship of Christ will at last be fully made visible, when all things will be finally reconciled in Christ and when all creation will be renewed, has led Baptists to certain actions in the present. This hope has constantly motivated Baptists to engage in evangelism, to oppose oppressive forces in society, and to be at the forefront of the promotion of social reforms which reflect the values of the coming Kingdom of God. In this generation, in face of pollution and destruction of the natural environment, they also recognise a new responsibility to care for the whole of creation.

APPENDIX C

Bibliography

This bibliography is a full, though not exhaustive, list of books and other material on Baptist identity published, with a few exceptions, in Great Britain.

The first section lists books and documents concerning Baptist principles in general. Sections then follow corresponding to the earlier chapter headings. This arrangement is designed to help the reader and in some cases titles should properly appear in more than one section.

Books marked with an asterisk are in print at time of publication. Many books and documents not in print are housed in the Angus Library in Regent's Park College, Oxford. The Angus Library is open to visitors by appointment (0865 59887).

GENERAL AND HISTORICAL

Amess, R., *One in the Truth?* (Kingsway, Eastbourne, 1988).

* *'Baptist Basics' series* published by the Baptist Union of Great Britain. See individual titles below.

  1. *The Blessing of Infants and the Dedication of Parents* by B. Green.
  2. *The Ministry of Deacons* by P. Beasley-Murray.
  3. *What is a Baptist Church?* by P. Wortley.
  4. *The Church Meeting – what is it?* by R. Hayden.
  5. *For those Visiting Applicants for Church Membership* by R. Mills.
  6. *Why Baptism and Church Membership?* by P. Beasley-Murray.
  7. *What do we do at the Lord's Supper?* by P. Beasley-Murray.

Baptist Union Documents 1948–1977 (Baptist Historical Society, 1980).
  – a compilation of reports issued by the Baptist Union of Great Britain and Ireland, selected and introduced by Roger Hayden. The reports included are:

  The Baptist Doctrine of the Church (1948).
  The Doctrine of the Ministry (1961).
  The Meaning and Practice of Ordination among Baptists (1957).
  Ministry Tomorrow (1969).
  The Report of the Commission on the Associations (1964).
  Working Together (1973).
  Baptists and Unity (1965).
  Visible Unity in Life and Mission (1977).
  The Child and the Church (1966).

Bebbington, D. W., *Baptist Convictions: a series of 9 topics for group study* (BU of Scotland, 1986).
* Brackney, W.H. (ed), *Faith, Life and Witness* – The Papers of the Study and Research Division of the Baptist World Alliance – 1986–1990 (Samford University, 1990, available from The Baptist Union, Didcot).
* Brown, R., *The English Baptists of the 18th Century* (Baptist Historical Society, 1986).
* Clements, K. W., *Baptists in the Twentieth Century* (Baptist Historical Society, London, 1963).
  Cook, H., *The Why of our Faith* (Kingsgate Press, London, n.d.).
  Cook, H., *What Baptists Stand For* (Carey Kingsgate Press, London, 1947).

Fiddes, P., 'The British Church Scene: Issues of identity for Baptists in discussion with others' (BWA Study Commissions, Montreal, 1991).

* Hayden, R., *English Baptist History and Heritage* (Baptist Union of Great Britain, Didcot, 1990).
* Haymes, B., *A Question of Identity: Reflections on Baptist Principles and Practice* (Yorkshire Baptist Association, Leeds, 1986).

McBain, D., *No Gentle Breeze: Baptist churchmanship and the winds of change* (Mainstream, 1981).

Overton, G., 'Baptist identity in terms of relationship': an unpublished lecture delivered to the Council of the European Baptist Federation, September 1990.

Payne, E.A., *The Fellowship of Believers: Baptist thought and practice yesterday and today* (Carey Kingsgate Press, London, 1944. Enlarged edition 1952).

Robinson, H. Wheeler, *The Life and Faith of the Baptists* (Carey Kingsgate Press, London, 1946. First published, Methuen, London, 1927).

Russell, D.S., *British Baptists Today: some questions concerning the Union and the churches*. (Baptist Union, London, 1971).

* Slater, D. (ed), *A Perspective on Baptist Identity* (Mainstream, 1987).

Underwood, A.C., *A History of the English Baptists* (Kingsgate Press, 1947).

Walton, R.C., *The Gathered Community* (Carey Press, London, 1946).

* West, M., *Baptist Principles* (Baptist Union, London, revised edition, 1967).
* White, B.R., *The English Baptists of the 17th Century* (Baptist Historical Society, 1983).

Wood, J., *The Baptists* (Pergamon Press, Oxford, 1977).

* Wright, N., *Challenge to Change: a radical agenda for Baptists* (Kingsway, Eastbourne, 1991).
* Yorkshire Baptist Association, *Fellowship in the Gospel: Six studies on Baptist principles & practice* (Leeds, 1989).

BAPTISM

Beasley-Murray, G.R., *Baptism Today and Tomorrow* (Macmillan, London, 1966).

* Beasley-Murray, G.R., *Baptism in the New Testament* (Macmillan, London, 1962; republished by Eerdmanns, Grand Rapids).
* Beasley-Murray, P., *Why Baptism and Church Membership?* (Baptist Basics series, Baptist Union, Didcot).

Burnish, R., *The Meaning of Baptism* (SPCK, London, 1985).

* Gordon, J.M., *Into Deep Water* (Baptist Union of Scotland, n.d.).
* Griffith, T., *The Case for Believers Baptism* (Kingsway, Eastbourne, 1990).

Matthews, J.F., *Baptism: a Baptist Viewpoint* (Baptist Union, London, 1976).

White, R.E.O., *The Biblical Doctrine of Initiation* (Hodder and Stoughton, 1966).

THE LORD'S SUPPER

* Beasley-Murray, P., *What do we do at the Lord's Supper?* (Baptist Basics series, Baptist Union, Didcot).

Childs, R.L., *The Lord's Supper* (Carey Kingsgate Press, London, 1951 and revised 1961).

Clark, N. *An Approach To The Theology Of The Sacraments* (SCM, London, 1956).

Davies, G.H., *Preaching the Lord's Supper* (London Baptist Preachers' Association, 1967).

* Walker, M., *Baptists at the Table: The Theology of the Lord's Supper amongst English Baptists in the Nineteenth Century* (Baptist Historical Society, 1992).
* Walker, M., *Preaching at the Lord's Table* (London Baptist Preachers' Association, 1988).

WORSHIP

* Baptist Union of Great Britain, *Patterns and Prayers for Christian Worship* (Oxford University Press, Oxford, 1991).
* Beasley-Murray, P., *Faith and Festivity: a guide for today's worship leaders* (MARC, Eastbourne, 1991).
  Clark, N. *Call To Worship* (SCM, London, 1960).
* Fiddes, P.S., *Charismatic Renewal: a Baptist Viewpoint* (Baptist Union, London, 1980).
  Gilmore, A., Smalley, E., Walker, M., *Praise God* (The Baptist Union, 1980).
* Green, B., *The Blessing of Infants and the Dedication of Parents* (Baptist Basics series, Baptist Union, Didcot).
  Payne, E.A., and Winward, S.F., *Orders and Prayers for Church Worship* (Baptist Union of Great Britain, revised edition 1965).
  Tennant, D.F., *Children in the Church: a Baptist View* (Baptist Union, London, 1978).
* Walker, M., *Infant Dedication* (Baptist Union, London, 1981).
* Wallace, J., *What happens in Worship?* (Baptist Union, London, 1982).
  Winward, S., *The Reformation of our Worship* (Carey Kingsgate Press, London, 1964).
  Winward, S., *Celebration and Order: a guide to worship and the lectionary* (Baptist Union, London, 1981).
  Yorkshire Baptist Association, *Christian Worship: some contemporary issues* (Leeds, 1984).

CHURCH MEMBERSHIP

* Beasley-Murray, P., *Why Baptism and Church Membership?* (Baptist Basics series, Baptist Union, Didcot).
* Clements, K.W., Kidd, R.L., Fiddes, P.S., Hayden, R., Haymes, B., *A Call to Mind* (Baptist Union, 1981).
* Fiddes, P.S., Hayden, R., Kidd, R.L., Clements, K.W., Haymes, B., *Bound to Love* (Baptist Union, 1985).
  Gilmore, A. (ed), *The Pattern of the Church: A Baptist View* (Lutterworth, London, 1963).
  Martin, G.W., *The Church: A Baptist View* (Baptist Union, London, 1976).
* Mills, R., *For those Visiting Applicants for Church Membership* (Baptist Basics series, Baptist Union, Didcot).
* Wortley, P., *What is a Baptist Church?* (Baptist Basics series, Baptist Union, Didcot).

AUTHORITY

* Baptist Union of Scotland, *Authority, Ministry & Business in the Church* (1985).
* Fiddes, P., *A Leading Question: the structure and authority of leadership in the local church* (Baptist Union, London, 1983).
* Hayden, R., *The Church Meeting – what is it?* (Baptist Basics series, Baptist Union, Didcot).
* White, B.R., *Authority: a Baptist View* (Baptist Union, London, 1976).

ASSOCIATING

* Baptist Union of Scotland, *Our Roman Catholic Neighbours* (n.d.).
Beasley-Murray, G.R., *Reflections on the Ecumenical Movement* (Baptist Union, London, 1965).
* Ellis, C. J., *Together on the Way: A Theology of Ecumenism* (BCC, London, 1990).
* Papers from the Commission on Baptist Doctrine and Interchurch Cooperation, in *Faith, Life and Witness* (see above for details).
Payne, E.A., *The Baptists of Berkshire* (Carey Kingsgate Press, London, 1951).

MINISTRY

Baptist Union of Scotland, *The Ministry Today* (n.d.).
Beasley-Murray, G.R., *Man and Woman in the Church* (Baptist Union, London, 1983).
* Beasley-Murray, P., *Dynamic Leadership* (MARC, Eastbourne, 1990).
* Beasley-Murray, P., *The Ministry of Deacons* (Baptist Basics series, Baptist Union, Didcot).
Nicholson, J.F.V., *The Ministry: a Baptist View* (Baptist Union, London, 1976).
* Papers from the Commissions on The Ministry and Laity and Pastoral Leadership, in *Faith, Life and Witness* (see above for details).

MISSION

* Amey, B., *The Unfinished Story* – a study-guide history of the Baptist Missionary Society (Baptist Union of Great Britain, 1991).
* Briggs, J.H.Y., *Freedom: a Baptist View* (Baptist Union, London, 1978).
* Monro, H., ed., *Witness Throughout the World* – seven studies on local and world evangelism based on the BWA Seoul Covenant (Baptist Union of Australia in conjunction with the BWA. Available from Baptist Union of Great Britain at Didcot).